THE BATTLE
OF MARSTON MOOR

THE BATTLE OF
MARSTON MOOR
1644

Peter Newman

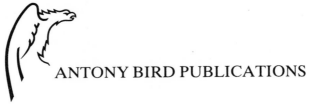

ANTONY BIRD PUBLICATIONS

First published in 1981 by
ANTONY BIRD PUBLICATIONS LTD
Strettington House, Strettington, Chichester

ISBN 0 907319 00 9

Designed by John Mitchell
Printed in Great Britain by
Clarke, Doble and Brendon
at Plymouth

CONTENTS

MAPS

LINE ILLUSTRATIONS

PLATES

All subjects courtesy National Portrait Gallery.
The plates are reproduced by courtesy of the National Portrait Gallery.

THE BATTLE
OF MARSTON MOOR

Introduction

MARSTON MOOR, or as local Royalists more frequently called it Hessay Moor, was, in terms of the number of men engaged, one of the largest battles ever fought on English soil. It was a battle so marked by extremes of courage and panic, by fluctuations in fortune, and by uncoordinated actions that it mirrors the events of the English Civil Wars in miniature. On Tuesday July 2nd 1644, in the space of few hours, the reputation of Prince Rupert received a stunning blow; the career of Oliver Cromwell was given a notable boost; and a fighting army, that of William Cavendish, Marquess of Newcastle, was virtually destroyed.

Prince Rupert's military career in England, and the legend of his invincibility, reinforced on the eve of battle by the relief of York, was never to recover from the blow. Fourteen months away lay the disgrace of the surrender of Bristol and the cashiering of numerous commanders linked irrevocably to the Prince's fate. The Marquess of Newcastle's northern regiments had set out, in early 1643, to overcome a resilient and efficient enemy, had triumphed in the summer of that year and then had seen their success frittered away in the wasteful siege of Hull. From January 1644, fighting on two fronts, to their north against the Scots, to the south against Parliamentarian forces given a much-needed breathing space by the Scots invasion, they had got into the habit of defeat. The battle of Selby, fought on April 11th 1644, emphasised this strikingly: Marston Moor confirmed it.

For the allied forces – Scots and English Parliamentarians – Marston Moor was enormously significant. For the Scots, it was their first taste of real battle since their invasion began in January 1644. They failed to capitalise on their contribution to the victory, and their cautious, unremarkable part in the remaining years of the war became the butt of caustic criticism from their English allies. The English forces of Parliament were the real victors at Marston Moor, and none more so than those of the Eastern Association army who looked not to their commander in chief, the Earl of Manchester, but to his Lieutenant General of the Horse, Oliver Cromwell. Cromwell, whose early political career at least was marked by a self-conscious reliance upon indications of divine approval or direction, saw in Marston Moor confirmation that he and the Godly Party were indeed in tune with the divine. Charles I and Oliver Cromwell had at least this in common: both

1

acted, as they believed, in conformity with God's will. For Cromwell, however, Marston Moor provided a fresh degree of certainty as to the rightness of his course of action at the same time as it merely served to increase the doubts of his superior, Manchester. In the carnage of the Yorkshire moorland was born the vitriolic dispute between Cromwell and Manchester, and the road from Marston Moor led directly to the New Model Army, to the assertion of Independency nascent in the Eastern Association army, and to military influence in the politics of the years 1646–1649.

THE HISTORIOGRAPHY

It is no wonder then that, of all the battles of the civil wars, none has received the attention accorded to Marston Moor. It features as the subject of scholarly monograph,[1] as a chapter in histories of the military aspect of the civil war,[2] and as a crucial part of tourist guides to English battlefields. It has drawn to it the precise, analytical mind of a C.H. Firth,[3] the amateur enthusiasm of an Alex Leadman,[4] and the vaguely antiquarian interests of retired professional soldiers, for example Alfred Burne and H. C. B. Rogers.[5] All have, to a greater or lesser extent, examined and interpreted the contemporary source materials, and some, notably A. H. Woolrych,[6] have endeavoured to relate documentary evidences to the terrain as it is today.

Yet not only do the numerous studies of the battle of Marston Moor testify to the importance of the engagement: they also indicate the degree to which what precisely happened on July 2nd 1644 remains a matter of historical opinion. The purpose of this present study is to explain what happened on that warm, wet summer evening by relating the contents of contemporary sources not only to one another, but, and essentially for a clearer understanding, to the nature of the terrain on which the battle was fought. It is also intended, while acknowledging their sometimes valuable contributions to the military history of the civil war, to avoid discussion of secondary studies. In other words, to tell the story of the battle from the viewpoint of the participants, making every attempt to see the terrain as they saw it, and to try to experience the vicissitudes of battle as they did. To dispense with secondary sources is one and the same thing as clearing away from the scene of battle the landscape changes of the last 300 years: it removes what has accumulated in the way of opinion, misunderstanding, factual error and myths in the creation and maintenance of which every writer on Marston Moor has unwittingly contributed. The very best studies of the battle, those of A. H. Burne, Austin Woolrych and Peter Young, and, of course, C. H. Firth, have contributed considerably to our knowledge of the military history of the civil wars. Where their work and that which is contained in this present study differ is in the matter of approach.

Detailed work on the battle and battlefield of Marston Moor began in 1973 and purely by chance. Living more or less on the battlefield, the present writer took the opportunity to familiarise himself with both the histories of the battle itself, and with the history of the landscape over which it was fought. Anomalies began to appear, and a programme of research was begun, based upon three main lines of study. Firstly, to examine all the contemporary or near contemporary sources relating to the events of July 2nd 1644, endeavouring to dismiss from their interpretation the received views of other writers. Secondly, to discover how and when the broad moorland of scrub and gorse and bog on which the battle had been fought was transformed into the neat, arable acreage which it now comprises, and, by charting the process of change, to attempt to arrive at a description of the vanished terrain. Thirdly, given the successful completion of these two lines of research, to draw them together so as to understand how it was that, for example, Sir Thomas Fairfax's raw cavalry regiments came to suffer such appalling losses.

This research involved a considerable degree of field work. With the active and interested approval of the landowners a systematic survey of the landscape at first hand was carried out. Every feature of the area of battle was familiarised, every hedgerow and track examined, and every yard of ground walked time after time. In the course of this survey, an additional source of information presented itself: artefacts. The soils of Marston and Hessay Moors are not conducive to the survival of metal, except in a badly corroded state, but lead shot is impervious to conditions which destroy steel, leather and cloth. Over the course of years it proved possible to chart extensive finds of musket shot and ultimately, from its distribution and type, to supplement the evidence of source and battlefield study. This additional material led conclusively towards a view of events markedly at variance with the interpretations of secondary writers. It had an additional value, as well, in that from the quality and diversity of relic material in general, it proved possible to draw conclusions about the equipment of the ordinary soldier present at the battle.

SOURCES

There are three groups of evidence available from the time of the battle which are used in this book. Group one, consisting entirely of written accounts, whether manuscript or printed, would include maps contemporary with events intended to illustrate troop dispositions and, if we are fortunate, aspects of terrain. This initial group must be further divided into a) primary sources written by participants within a month or so of the events which they are describing; b) what might be called secondary/primary sources written by participants or by others at their behest, sometimes many years later; and c) secondary news sources, written for popular circulation, or contained in private correspondence between non-combatants and based upon received eye-witness accounts or not (it is often hard to distinguish). Group two consists of that evidence relating solely to the terrain itself, or of those sources already comprised in the gradations of group one which cast light upon specific terrain features. We would recognise here estate maps, enclosure awards and maps, regional and area maps drafted between, say, 1600 and the first edition of the Ordnance Survey, tithe maps, leases and deeds, agricultural drainage records and plans, and other documentary material relating to the history of the land itself. Group three involves the field work and artefact discovery and interpretation alluded to earlier, the study of the features of the landscape 'in situ' and the application of Alfred Burne's I.M.P. – Inherent Military Probability'.

Lt.-Colonel James Somerville's account[7] of the battle contains the following observation:

> The order of this great battle, wherein both armies was near of an equal number . . . I shall not take upon me to describe; albeit from the draughts then taken upon the place and information I received from this gentleman, who being then a volunteer, as having no command, had opportunity and liberty to ride from the one wing of the army to the other, to view all their several squadrons of horse and battalions of foot, how formed, and in what manner drawn up, with every other circumstance relating to this fight, and that both as to the king's armies and that of the parliament's. . . .

Somerville, whose account is classified as primary/secondary in that it is received information from an eye-witness, throws out a tantalising hint. He alludes to the 'draughts then taken upon the place': indicating that he had seen sketch maps or plans of troop dispositions. Only two such are known to exist, those of de Gomme[8] and Lumsden:[9] the latter shows allied dispositions but no terrrain features, whilst the former shows both but is open to critical reinterpretation (see Chapters 2 and 3). Since it is unlikely that Somerville was shown de Gomme's plan, and only remotely possible that he saw Lumsden's, clearly other 'draughts' no longer extant existed. How detailed these were we have no way of knowing, although Somerville when he wrote assumed familiarity on the part of his interested readers. Whether any of these 'draughts' might have been salvaged during the last century is a purely academic point: it is almost certainly the lack of any comparative plans which has led to the importance attached to de Gomme and from that importance to the basic assumption that de Gomme's plan of Royalist dispositions is a fundamental source from which to begin a study. In point of fact, it is somewhat misleading: but when that is realised, the problem of Marston Moor is not intensified, but eased.

The strictly primary sources upon which this study is based (full details of each of which are set out in the bibliography) are those of Simeon Ashe (referred to henceforth as Ashe), William Stewart, Robert Douglas (referred to as Douglas), Thomas Stockdale, Lionel Watson, Thomas Fairfax, W. H., William Fairfax, and Sir James Lumsden for the allied side (including the official but in fact uninformative allied generals' despatch): and those of Sir Henry Slingsby, Sir Philip Monckton and, with care, that of de Gomme, for the Royalists. Primary/secondary sources are those of Mr. Ogden, the Rupert Diary, the Newcastle Memoirs, Sir Hugh Cholmeley for the Royalists: and those of Somerville and William Lilly for the allies.

The secondary sources, as earlier defined, are those of Edward Bowles, Robert Clarke, Arthur Trevor, Edmund Ludlow, Henry Shelley, Lord Saye, ?William Savage, Mrs. Alice Thornton and John Vicars.

Historians have varied in the importance which they have attached to the various sources. Thus, all have agreed on the importance of de Gomme since C. H. Firth published the plan in 1898, whilst attaching little importance to the account by Captain William Stewart, *A Full Relation of the Victory Obtained*, written on 6th July 1644; dismissing it as a composite account, alluding to its apparent confusion. Even Burne did not understand the implications of this tract. The case of the Stewart source is a prime example of the way in which a study of changes in terrain can elucidate otherwise mystifying allusions, and the real importance of Stewart is established in Chapter 5. Those who have dismissed him as interesting but muddled, have hamstrung their own efforts to interpret the dangerous situation in which Sir Thomas Fairfax's cavalry found themselves on the allied right wing at the onset of the battle. Charles Sanford Terry, a neglected but extremely able military historian, in his study of the allied commander in chief, the Earl of Leven,[10] made much use of Stewart's account, and although he failed to give it its full due, even so, no writer since has treated it so seriously. Alfred Burne was much exercised by details contained in the account, but clearly did not dwell upon it long enough to reach a solution. Had he even glanced at the map of the battlefield suplied by S. R. Gardiner in his first·volume of the history of the civil wars,[11] a solution might have suggested itself, but that criticism applies to others as much as to Burne.

Some comment is also called for on the primary/secondary source of Sir Hugh Cholmeley's 'Memorials touching the battle of York', published in 1890. Cholmeley himself was a renegade from the Parliamentarian army,[12] having gone over to the King in early 1643 and retaining control, as part of the bargain which he struck with the Queen and the Earl of Newcastle, of Scarborough Castle. He was the host, on July 3rd, to the northern generals who chose to accompany Newcastle into exile. In other words, within a day or two at most of the battle, Cholmeley heard eye-witness accounts of events there, and not only from those who might be supposed to have shared the criticism which Newcastle is said to have made of Prince Rupert's decision to fight a battle at all. Newcastle's escort to Scarborough, given to him by Prince Rupert, was commanded by a Kent gentleman, Colonel Sir John Mayney of Linton, Baronet,[13] who, although no other histories of the battle take account of it, was in fact a Brigade commander at Marston Moor. Thus Cholmeley had opportunity to hear at first-hand two or more disparate views of the same engagement, and his record of what he heard, though cast in the form of animadversions for the Earl of Clarendon to draw upon some years later, is crucial. During the months after Marston Moor until Scarborough fell to storm in July 1645, it provided a safe refuge for Royalist officers whose regiments had broken up in the north. Henry Constable, Viscount Dunbar, who was killed defending Scarborough,[16] had fought on Marston Moor in the cavalry regiment of the Northumbrian Catholic, Sir Edward Widdrington of Cartington.[17] He is but one of several examples of persons well placed to give an account of the battle to Cholmeley, and this underlines the significance of Sir Hugh's version of events. Moreover, it is not apparent that Cholmeley had any political or personal axe to grind so that we may say with some certainty that his was an objective analysis of what he had been told.

The narrative of Mr. Ogden, also a primary/secondary source, is similarly important although less detailed. Ogden was writing to Sir Walter Wrottesley on July 6th, and his letter is endorsed

> This is verbatim as much as I could remember of Dr. Lewins lre to his wife: who himselfe had beene taken but for his strong horse and his rotten spanner string.

It is a pity that Dr. Lewins' letter itself has not survived; he was a royalist cavalryman in the very thick of the fighting. In a melee, he had evidently been surrounded by the enemy, one or some of whom had made to pull him from his horse, and had seized upon the thong by which the spanner for winding his wheel-lock pistol was attached to his belt. The horse, pulling against the efforts of the enemy, had caused the thong to snap, thus permitting Lewins to escape. His escape was fortuitous in providing a further eye-witness account of events, albeit recorded by a third party with qualifications as to his memory. We do not know where Mrs. Lewins was to receive her husband's letter, but clearly she was not in York (it was not unusual for wives to accompany their husbands on campaign), so that Dr. Lewins must have written his letter within a day or so of the battle. It is this aspect which makes Ogden's narrative of more immediate importance than the letter of Henry Shelley, written in London on 9th July 1644, to Sir Thomas Pelham, which is classified as secondary because it is full of received information without evidence that this had come from an eye-witness, which would have been improbable anyway at that date and at that distance.

A potentially valuable source, the letter from Sir William Fairfax, a Parliamentarian commander, to his wife, written on July 3rd from Long Marston itself, and certainly primary, is disappointing. It concerns details with which Mrs. Fairfax would have been familiar, concerning individuals and her husband's condition, but offers nothing more substantial. Numerous letters written by participants fortunate enough to have come off unscathed, or at least able to write, must have been penned in the few days after the battle, and it may be that at some stage at least one, hitherto unknown, will come to light.

ACKNOWLEDGEMENTS

Whilst the author is, of course, responsible in their entirety for the conclusions reached in the course of this work, it will be evident that a debt of gratitude is due to many others who facilitated or materially assisted in the research. The landowners of Marston Moor were, on the whole, tolerant of and interested in the process of field walking. Special thanks must be extended to Mr. Richard Barnitt, Mr. Richard Burniston and Mr. J. Q. Midgley, and these three must be permitted to stand for many others, farmers and farmworkers, who contributed information and advice over the years. Thanks are also due to Arthur Credland, Keeper of Exhibitions at the Town Docks Museum, Hull, who put his expertise in early military equipment at my disposal: Nigel Arch, Keeper of Military History at the Castle Museum, York: Dr. Keith Manchester of the School of Archaeological Sciences at the University of Bradford and his colleague Arnold Aspinall: Mr. John Knapton of Bradford: David Jenkins of the Department of Biology, University College of North Wales: and to Richard Stansfield of the Castle Museum, York, and Mr. J. S. Illsley for their photographs.

However, no expression of gratitude, however effusive, could truly acknowledge the assistance given by Victor Cammidge of Hessay, to whom this book is dedicated. From 1975 to the present, he has put in hours of his free time in field work and in appraisal of the writer's ideas and theories. His keen attention to detail and his thorough and cautious assessment of findings is impressive: and if, in the last analysis, this work reflects my own view on minor points on which we have agreed to differ, it is because the conclusions must stand or fall on the writer's merits alone.

Research is a lonely business, and something to which the historian is by calling accustomed. Field work too has that quality. Those many friends and interested persons who opted to accompany the writer on foot across Marston Moor in the dead of winter, as well as in the height of summer, deserve their share of thanks. Not least of these, my wife, who came, as I did, to enjoy the moor whatever the season, and for whom familiarity with the landscape has bred undying affection.

P. R. Newman

UCNW

NOTES

1. Young, P., *Marston Moor 1644*, Kineton 1970.
2. See, for example, Burne, A. H., & Young, P., *The Great Civil War*, 1959; and Holmes, R., & Young, P., *The English Civil War*, 1974.
3. Firth, C. H., 'Marston Moor', *Transactions of the Royal Historical Society*, New Series, Vol. XII, 1898.
4. Leadman, A. D. H., *Battles Fought in Yorkshire*, 1891.
5. Burne, A. H., *The Battlefields of England*, 1950. Rogers, H. C. B., *Batles and Generals of the Civil Wars*, 1968.
6. Woolrych, A. H., *Battles of the English Civil War*, 1961.
7. James Lord Somerville, *Memorie of the Somervilles*, Edinburgh 1815, Vol. II, pp. 343/352.
8. Sir Bernard de Gomme's 'Order of His Maj[ties] Armee', was published by C. H. Firth, op. cit., f.n. 3, and is in British Library Additional Ms. 16370, f. 64.
9. Sir James Lumsden's plan and letter is in the archives of York Minster Library.
10. Terry, C. S., *The Life and Campaigns of Alexander Leslie First Earl of Leven*, 1899.
11. Gardiner, S. R., *History of the Great Civil War*, 1904, Vol. I, p. 375.
12. For Cholmeley's career, see Dictionary of National Biography; G.E.C., ed: *Complete Baronetage*, Vol. II, p. 128; Sir Hugh Cholmeley, *The Memoirs of Sir Hugh Cholmeley*, 1787.
13. Anon, 'The Services Performed by Sir John Mayne of Linton', Alnwick Castle Archives.
14. G.E.C., *Complete Peerage*, Vol. IV, p. 513. Dictionary of National Biography.
15. G.E.C., *Complete Baronetage*, Vol. II, p. 188. *Calendar of State Papers, Domestic Series*, 1660/1661, p. 339.

The Main Events

Chapter 1

THE CONTEXT:
THE WAR IN THE NORTH

January – June 1644

PRINCE RUPERT'S raising of the siege of York on June 30th 1644 brought a much needed, but false, promise of a recovery of fortunes for the hard pressed northern Royalist army. Two days, later, hope was wrecked in a battle that might have been avoided and that certainly need not then have been fought. Prince Rupert saw that three enemy armies had been driven in some degree of demoralisation from before the walls of the northern capital, and it was his intention to destroy them while he possessed what we would call the psychological advantage. That he failed was due to a number of reasons, but that failure brought to an abrupt end a chapter of the military history of the civil war, putting paid to the existence of a recognisable northern army. The battle of Marston Moor was fought as a direct consequence of the need to relieve the city of York, and that the situation in Yorkshire had come to so perilous a condition was itself the result of months of steady Royalist defeat and retreat.

From January 1644 two wars were fought in the north; between the Royalists and the Scots in the wastes of Northumberland and Durham, and between the Royalists and a resurgent Parliamentarian presence in Yorkshire and along that county's southern and western borders. In these two theatres of war, and particularly in that of Yorkshire, were laid the seeds of defeat on Marston Moor, a fact which is only clearly understood by a survey of the military history of the winter and spring of that year.[1]

THE WAR AGAINST THE SCOTS, JANUARY TO APRIL 1644.

For a monthly subsidy, agreed in negotiations between the Parliament and Scottish representatives in September 1643, the Scots put into the field an army which was to draw the forces of the Marquess of Newcastle away north. The year 1643 had been on the whole throughout England a bleak one for the Parliament, markedly so in the north and the north midlands. From June 30th when the Yorkshire army of Lord Fairfax had been decisively routed at Adwalton Moor near Bradford, Parliamentarian forces had been on the defensive, squeezed out of their recruiting grounds of the West Riding and forced into Lincolnshire or into the garrison port of Hull. Failure to take Hull had been the first, but not in itself major, setback for the successful Royalists, and in the wake of that, Newcastle had led a sweeping campaign into Derbyshire and Nottinghamshire which had re-emphasised the qualities of his army. The dread felt in London of a southward thrust by the Marquess to link up with the Oxford army in a pincer movement on London, made the conclusion of an agreement with the Scots more than imperative. Whether or not the Royalist high command in the north seriously contemplated such a strategy is not relevant to the assumptions upon which Parliament's policy was based, and certainly the bringing in of the Scots rendered any potential southern advance by the Royalists out of the question.

Sir Philip Warwick[2] claimed that although Newcastle had been given forewarning of a Scottish invasion, he did nothing to prepare against it. This was not true. In November 1643 Sir Thomas Glemham,[3] governor of York and Colonel-General of the Yorkshire forces, had been sent to Newcastle-upon-Tyne to supervise defence plans and to organise Northumbrian forces against the impending invasion. It might be the case that the Marquess could see no reason for a Scottish invasion, as Warwick also claimed, but if that is so it did not mean that he was not going to prepare against the unlikely. If anything, Newcastle felt his army to be sufficient of a threat in itself to deter the Scots from acting, and it is the case that until Marston Moor was fought the Scots managed to avoid involving themselves in a major battle against veteran Royalist units.

The Scots appeared at Berwick on January 18th with 18,000 Foot, 3,000 Horse, 500 Dragoons and a train of artillery of 120 guns, whilst ships ferried supplies into Berwick.[4] Newcastle, who hurried back into Yorkshire from Welbeck, his Nottinghamshire home, now had to deal rapidly with the unlikely eventuality which had come to pass. Relying upon Glemham and the commanders in Northumberland to hinder the enemy advance for a time, the Marquess issued orders calling his regiments out of winter quarters, and arraying additional forces.[5] He had to leave behind him in Yorkshire enough men to maintain what had been won in 1643, whilst taking with him sufficient of his veteran army to bring the Scots rapidly to battle and put an end to their incursion. His cavalry, about 3,000 strong, was equal in number and superior in experience to the Scots but as he told Prince Rupert in a letter of 28th January[6] 'truly I cannot march five thousand foot', a reflection of the need to defend Yorkshire, from which county most of his infantry had been raised. By issuing new commissions to loyal gentry in North Yorkshire and Durham he might hope to double the size of the foot at his disposal, but would inevitably dilute his veterans with raw companies. Commissions of array were sent out to raise the Trained Bands in North Yorkshire (the civilian militia forces narrowly parochial in their outlook, and largely superseded by volunteer regiments during the course of the war), instructing them to join the Marquess on his march north.[7]

In Northumberland Sir Thomas Glemham, with his headquarters at Alnwick Castle, kept careful watch on Scottish movements. Colonel Sir Francis Anderson,[8] well forward at Wooler, sent detailed reports back to base. At Oxford, the preparations against the Scots were looked upon as adequate to cope with the threat, and the jocularity with which Royalists there spoke of 'those holy Pilgrims come lately into Northumberland',[9] did not square with the cold, winter reality in the distant north. Glemham found that weather conditions and the non-appearance of reinforcements from Yorkshire obliged him to evacuate Alnwick and to fall back on Newcastle-upon-Tyne, destroying bridges as he went. Snow was followed by rain 'which so swell'd the waters' that the Scottish infantry, pushing remorselessly on, crossed streams 'up to their middle, and sometimes to the arme-pits'.[10]

On January 28th the Marquess of Newcastle set off north, and on that day the Scots took Morpeth. Glemham, from Newcastle upon Tyne, sent out commissions 'yt all men were warned to goe against ye Scotts',[11] but with variable success. The race to see who would reach the Tyne port, the Scots from the north, or the Royalists pushing up through Durham, was won by the Marquess with twelve hours to spare.[12] On February 3rd the Earl of Leven appeared before the town,

15

and summoned it to surrender. Receiving the defiance of the Mayor and Council, he launched an assault upon a defensive sconce, but the Scots were driven off with severe losses[13] by Colonel Charles Slingsby, who was himself to die on Marston Moor.

It was apparent to the Marquess that the garrison of Newcastle was more then adequate to maintain the port, and, since his primary strength lay in his veteran cavalry, it was pointless remaining within the walls. His horse regiments were commanded into action to disrupt any attempt to cross the Tyne on the part of the Earl of Leven and on February 19th, in a pitched fight at Corbridge, Scottish and Royalist cavalry met in an action that was a foretaste of Marston Moor. Despite some Royalist losses, Sir Marmaduke Langdale[14] secured a victory, and 200 Scottish prisoners were despatched to York to cheer the garrison there.[15] In fact, however, Corbridge was a warning to the Earl of Leven not to commit his hardy but raw cavalry to pitched battle if he wanted to keep his army intact. Sir James Turner, a career soldier with the Scots at this juncture, observed:

> I looked upon this armie of the Scots (of which the Parliament so much boasted) . . . I found the bodies of the men lustie, well clothed and well moneyd, bot raw, untrained and undisciplined: their officers for most part young and unexperienced.[16]

Turner felt that had the Marquess been able to bring the Scots to battle the outcome had been inevitable, and added that he felt part of the failure to do this rested with Newcastle's principal advisor, James King, Baron Eythin, a man whose role, as General of the Foot in the northern army, was crucial to the outcome of the battle of Marston Moor. 'He was a person of great honor,' wrote Turner, 'but what he had saved of it . . . in Germanie, where he had made a shipwracke of much of it, he lost in England.'[17] Yet even had James King been less cautious than he undoubtedly was, nothing could have overcome Leven's awareness of the limitations of the Scottish army and his commitment to avoidance of any confrontation that might have put paid to the invasion once and for all. The importance of the northern war was increasing daily as the Marquess of Newcastle received reports from Yorkshire, and every day that the Scottish army remained intact was a blow against the King's party north of Trent. 'Absolutely the seat of war will be in the north,' the Marquess wrote on February 13th, 'a great army about Newark behind us, and the great Scotch army before us.'[18] It was an unenviable position.

The siege of Newcastle proving fruitless and undermining such morale as the Scottish army possessed, the Earl of Leven decided to abandon it, leaving behind a few regiments, and to press on southwards to effect a junction with the Parliamentarian army in Yorkshire. Bad weather hampered counter-action by the Royalists, a blizzard on February 21st, 'a terrible storm of drift and snow' on the 24th, and on the 28th the Scottish army forced the crossing of the Tyne at three points. On March 4th Sunderland was entered. Durham, however, was a hostile county far more than Northumberland had been, 'soe great a power hath the cathedral here' complained one Scot.[19] In crossing the Tyne Leven had taken a gamble with his army, entering a major recruitment ground for the Royalist army, and stretching his lines of communication seriously in the foul weather conditions of that winter. For the Royalists it could be said that although they had been obliged to abandon Northumberland, Newcastle-upon-Tyne stood firm, and the few pitched fights between them and the enemy had resulted in Royalist success. All depended upon the Marquess being able to force Leven into a major battle. Reinforcements had come in from Durham, and 2,000 men had marched across from Cumberland[20] increasing the Royalist infantry. On March 7th and 8th was, almost, fought the battle which was needed.

The battle of the Bowden Hills was marked by the tactical skill of the Earl of Leven, who drew his army up in inaccessible places, and the frustration of the Marquess of Newcastle.[21] On the 7th, Leven's forces were so well positioned on a height and covered by serious obstacles of terrain, that to bring them to battle, as the Marquess observed, 'we must have fetched so great a compass about, that they would have been upon the same hill again to have received us that way'. On the 8th the snow fell so heavily that further thoughts of attack uphill were shelved, while there was some concern for the Royalist cavalry, whose horses for a third day 'had received little or no sustenance'; the bitter cold undermined veteran infantry who had grown to despair of fighting an enemy 'so hard to be provoked'. The Royalists withdrew, occasioning an attempt by Leven to try to engage their rearguard, but the attempt was an ignominious failure.

During the early part of March, reinforcements from Yorkshire had arrived in the shape of two cavalry regiments commanded overall by Sir Charles Lucas, recently appointed Lt.-General of the Horse to the

Marquess. Even allowing for losses and desertions this brought the Royalist cavalry in the field to at least 5,000 including forces drawn from Northumberland, Durham and Cumbria. In view of the strategy employed by Leven, however, Lucas would have been better employed in Yorkshire, where he had initially been in January and February. It is not clear whether Newcastle actually ordered Lucas up to him, or whether the latter acted on his own authority, but it is certainly evident that the depletion of the Yorkshire cavalry at this stage had serious repercussions for the defence of that county, as will be seen. The Royalists fell back on Durham city, the Scots returned to Sunderland, awaiting supplies and fortifying it as a base camp. It seems now to have become the Royalist objective to rest and recuperate, ready to bar the way south should Leven take the offensive once more. Yet all these considerations rested upon the situation in the Royalist rear, which the Marquess did not dwell upon in his occasional despatches to Oxford. King Charles commended the actions of the northern high command: 'I judge the Scots rebelles to be in much worse case, than your army', and urged that he be notified of events at least once a week 'indeed twyce would doe better'.[22] This letter, betraying the anxiety felt at Oxford, was written in mid-March. On March 24th Leven's army moved.

Hitherto contained more or less in the area north of the River Wear, voraciously eating up their forage such as it was, the Scots now needed to occupy fresh ground. Retreat into Northumberland was out of the question, and since the only way was forward, Leven opted for it. The Royalist commanders, aware of all such developments, attempted to block his route at Hilton and bring him to battle at long last.[23] The battle of Hilton was virtually a replay of that at Bowden Hills, and roughly on the same sort of ground, but this time Leven was more willing to fight. The slaughter was prodigious, and concerned chiefly the infantry of the two armies, but the sifting of occasionally contradictory reports suggests that while losses on both sides were heavy (and the Royalists least able to bear them), the battle was more or less a stalemate. However, Leven withdrew his men to Sunderland, which was now fortified with artillery in position, and on the 25th this artillery drove off an attempted storm by the Royalists. The latter in their turn pulled back, were set upon by Scottish cavalry and these, in their turn, routed by Sir Charles Lucas. The battle emphasised the Royalist deficiency in infantry, of which the Marquess had first complained in late January. The latter wrote to Rupert:

> I must assure your Highness that the Scots are as big again in foot as I
> am . . . so that if your Highness do not please to come hither, and that
> very soon too, the great game of your uncle's will be endangered, if no
> lost.[24]

This was written on the 25th, and sent in the hands of Colonel Sir John
Mayney.[25] The consistency of Newcastle's view of the northern war as a
crucial aspect of the whole is emphasised, and the requests for aid from
Rupert clearly pre-date the period of the siege of York by some time.
On the day after the letter was sent, Newcastle and his staff decided to
retreat across the face of Durham and to head for the line of the River
Tees, almost certainly to make that the last line of resistance, the scene
of the first victory of the northern army in 1642. The Scots however now
drew closer to Durham city, occupying Quarrendon Hill, and until April
12th the two armies faced each other with little or no skirmishing. On
the 12th came news that destroyed all of the Marquess's strategic and
tactical resolutions: on that day he heard of the disastrous defeat
sustained by the Yorkshire army at Selby on the previous day, April
11th. There was only one objective now, to re-run the race of January,
but this time to get to York and save the northern capital before the
victorious Parliamentarians could capture it.

This was a race against time, for not only had the Yorkshire army
been virtually destroyed at Selby, but the Yorkshire commander in
chief, John Belasyse, governor of York, had been taken prisoner with
many of his staff. There was a vacuum in the Yorkshire high command,
and only Newcastle himself could fill it. The Scots were suddenly a
secondary menace. The problem was to bring the army, more or less
intact, into York. The campaign against the Scots had been lost.

> That formidable Popish Armie of the Marquis of Newcastell, which was
> the greatest in England when our armie went in, hes beene so closelie
> followed as a great part of his forces both foot and horse, ar ather killed,
> takin, run away, & disbanded.[26]

This piece of Scottish propaganda contains a morsel of truth. However
skilful the retreat into Yorkshire was, it was carried out at speed, and
this speed meant that numerous infantry units either gave up or were
left behind. Regiments raised in Durham earlier in the year to fight the
Scots, raw and untrained as the Scots themselves, were indeed
disbanded. A few veteran Durham regiments managed to extricate

themselves and get into Yorkshire, but they lost men in skirmishes as the Scots followed in the rear. Of course, the Scots had never had to face the full strength of the northern field army: throughout the campaign they had outnumbered Newcastle in infantry at least two to one, although the edge in numbers in cavalry had by mid-March been in Newcastle's favour. Not that it mattered, for he had had no chance to use them to effect.

Newcastle entered York unopposed on April 14th/15th, sending his cavalry forces away south and west to give them opportunity to operate. On the 16th, the Scottish army occupied Thornaby on Tees, and two days later came to Wetherby where they at last linked up with the Parliament's army under Sir Thomas Fairfax. On April 22nd the siege of York began.

THE WAR IN YORKSHIRE JANUARY TO APRIL 1644.

The departure of the governor of York, Sir Thomas Glemham, to supervise defensive preparations in Northumberland, in November 1643, brought to a temporary end his long relationship with the city since his appointment as governor in October 1642. He was replaced by a local man, Colonel Sir William Saville of Thornhill,[27] upon whose shoulders the Marquess expected command in Yorkshire to devolve. Superficially Yorkshire was in solid Royalist control, with the exception of Hull, the raiding cavalry of which under Thomas Fairfax had gone into Lincolnshire in autumn 1643 and so on into Cheshire. Sir Francis Mackworth[28] held the West Riding in a firm grip and fended off punitive forays from across the Pennines in Parliamentary Lancashire. The Scottish invasion did not in itself undo all that had been achieved: it provoked a crisis in Yorkshire which was further aggravated by the sudden death of Sir William Saville on January 22nd. The latter had been a moderate, competent field commander, and if Glemham had had a hand in appointing him as his successor this argues for Saville's capabilities. His replacement, rapidly appointed, was a different proposition altogether.

John Belasyse[29] was 30 years of age, a Catholic and a younger son whose marriage would take him a step towards the peerage conferred in 1645 which he richly deserved. His experience had been as an active field commander with the Oxford army, where he had distinguished himself. It is not clear precisely why he was appointed to replace Saville, nor is it clear whether this was at the instigation of the Marquess, of Prince Rupert, or the King himself: we do not even know if Belasyse wanted the job. Yet, on 28th January, he was installed as governor of York and commander in chief in Yorkshire in Newcastle's absence, with some very loosely defined orders to maintain Royalist control:

> the governor . . . left behind with sufficient forces for the defence of that country . . . had orders not to encounter the enemy, but to keep himself in a defensive posture.[30]

This was implicit in Newcastle's decision to take virtually all his cavalry north with him, leaving behind probably half of the infantry of the army, perhaps 5,000 men, or roughly speaking five to six regiments. These were supported by a few cavalry regiments at less than half strength, chiefly West Riding forces or the remains of regiments originally formed in Lancashire in early 1643 and driven from their home base by Parliamentarian success. The arrival of Sir Charles Lucas, sent from Prince Rupert with 1,000 or so additional cavalry, gave the Marquess an opportunity to strengthen this arm of the Yorkshire army but, as has been seen, by early March Lucas and his contingent had moved into Durham. Given this limited military muscle it remained to be seen how Belasyse would interpret his orders. To act defensively was not the same thing as avoiding battle: indeed, battle might be the best defensive move under certain circumstances. This is clearly how Belasyse saw things, and if he was proved wrong in his expectations, in his judgements he was not seriously at fault.

John Belasyse was an efficient commander, as he was to prove as governor of Newark on Trent in late 1645. Immediately upon arrival in Yorkshire he began to draw loosely quartered regiments together and to create some semblance of cohesion.[31] Making use of the presence of Lucas, he distributed his cavalry into three commands, one at Leeds for the West Riding, a second at Malton to cover the East Riding, and a third at York to serve as cover for the North Riding and as back-up for the other two commands. His foot were distributed at crucial garrisons – Halifax, Doncaster, Leeds and Stamford Bridge. Yet as well as preserving Yorkshire, Belasyse was obliged to maintain lines of communication with the army in the field against the Scots, and to ferry north supplies of men, materials and food: 'no difficulty could possibly be greater to any person in His Majesty's service', observed Belasyse's secretary.

Sometime between February 9th and 20th, the Parliamentarians in Hull began the process by which Belasyse's thin covering of forces was exploited. Sir William Constable

> crept out of Hull wth their Horse, making their Carrocols upon ye Woulds, & was heard of as far as Pickering. Against him Collonell Belasyse sends all our horse, & some foot, together wth Sr Charles Lucas, to fource him to keep within Hull, or else to fight him.[32]

The Royalist cavalry split up to hunt him down, and on the night of either February 10th or 14th Constable descended on a part of the cavalry and badly mauled them in their quarters. One of the regiments attacked belonged to Colonel Sir Walter Vavasour,[33] and the experiences of his regiment now and in April illustrates the progressive destruction of Belasyse's field army in Yorkshire. In the wake of this action, Constable took Bridlington, dangerously close to the Royalist garrison of Scarborough,[34] scored a victory at Driffield, and capured Whitby with its tiny garrison.[35]

The abject failure of the Royalists to counter this sally from Hull increased enemy confidence, and reflects the difficulties confronting John Belasyse. Determined not to be so out-manouevred again, Colonel Belasyse took the field in early March to block a Parliamentarian incursion into the West Riding aimed at the seizure and occupation of Bradford, a town of markedly anti-Royalist sympathies. Colonel John Lambert[36] had been detached from the army of Sir Thomas Fairfax, then operating in Cheshire and in south Lancashire, and sent back into Yorkshire to take what advantage he could of propitious circumstances. Lambert saw Bradford as a good base from which to penetrate deeper into Royalist territory, and a base in an area friendly to his soldiers, many of whom were West Riding men. The action at Bradford was brief,[37] Royalist presence there being insufficient to resist veteran troops fighting on their home soil, and the town was occupied. On March 6th, moving out from his base, Lambert attacked a Royalist cavalry force at Hunslet[38] and scored another victory over at least three cavalry regiments which had begun their civil war careers in Lancashire, two of them certainly the regiments of Sir William Bradshaw of the Haigh and Sir George Middleton of Leighton, both of which fought on Marston Moor.

Whilst all this was happening, Belasyse was moving men and supplies to Leeds, hastening the reorganisation he had begun in early

February to meet the threat from the west. Unable to prevent the occupation of Bradford as he had hoped, his task now was to contain and, if it might be done, reverse the situation. The fact is, the initiative had slipped decidedly into the Parliament's favour. To recover it Belasyse determined upon a short, sharp defensive campaign in the West Riding. He

> drew all his troops together and rendezvous at Selby, where he formed a small array of 5,000 foot and 1,500 horse, and marched in person from York to command them, with six pieces of cannon and a train. At Selby he made a bridge of boats over the river Ouse to communicate with the East Riding; from hence he marched 1,000 foot and 500 horse to attack Bradford. . . .

In selecting Selby as an operational headquarters, on a strategic line giving access towards Hull and into the West Riding, John Belasyse was displaying sound strategic thinking if he could succeed in disrupting Lambert's control around Bradford. If he could not achieve that, and worse still, if he were beaten, Selby would be vulnerable to a concerted move from Hull and the west. To strengthen his hand, he sought and found help in Nottinghamshire where, on March 21st, Prince Rupert had raised the siege of Newark and outmanoevred the Parliamentarian army. This help consisted of forces under the command of Colonel Gervase Lucas from Belvoir Castle, and some of Rupert's own men under the thoroughly incompetent George Porter.[39] Porter was to fight on Marston Moor. In view of the psychological impact of the relief of Newark, Belasyse, with this additional help, could seriously hope to dislodge Lambert and re-establish the status quo which had prevailed in Yorkshire when he assumed his command. On March 25th Bradford was attacked.

Accounts of the action are few and confused[40] but it seems that after several hours fighting the defenders under Lambert made a desperate attempt to break through, forced back George Porter, and made good their escape. Darkness intervening and ammunition running low, Belasyse fell back on Leeds, his Lancashire cavalry again sustaining losses. The failure to destroy Lambert, and Porter's immediate departure into Nottinghamshire to sulk,[41] put Selby in grave risk. For, while the second engagement at Bradford was being fought out, Sir Thomas Fairfax and his army from Cheshire, reinforced with some Lancashire units, was moving back towards Yorkshire, summoned by

Ferdinando Lord Fairfax.[42] Father and son met at Ferrybridge and Sir Thomas, disregarding orders from London to move rapidly into Durham to assist the Scots, agreed to a joint attack on Selby. Sir Thomas had at his disposal 2,000 cavalry, not counting infantry; Lord Fairfax cannot have had less than that in foot, and perhaps 1,000 horse; whilst Sir John Meldrum,[43] who had extricated his army relatively intact from before Newark, marched up from the Isle of Axholm to join with them. Belasyse had at Selby the army of 6,500 men, probably weakened by losses, with which he had first occupied that town. Appeals for assistance had gone unheeded: George Porter and Henry Hastings, Lord Loughborough[44] ordered to his aid, did not materialise. From March 28th until April 11th Belasyse waited at Selby and waited in vain, while the enemy organised and grew in strength. The battle that ensued was the 'fatal blow' the 'very dawning of yt day which brought prosperous success' to the Parliament, as one Royalist put it.[45]

To remove John Belasyse and the Yorkshire army, such as it was, would be to remove the only obstacle between an effective conjunction of the armies of the Parliament and of the Scots. Whether or not Belasyse should have clung on to Selby or should have fallen back on York is irrelevant: he stayed at Selby and, in the course of a battle that raged for several hours in the streets of that little country town, his army was destroyed, and he himself, wounded several times, captured and taken to Hull. Colonel Sir Walter Vavasour, whose cavalry regiment had been mauled at the onset of the resurgence of Parliamentarian strength in the county, was also wounded, escaped, and got into York where the deputy governor Henry Wait[46] held temporary control. Vavasour was so badly wounded that he secured permission from the Marquess of Newcastle to leave and take himself into Europe from where, later in the year, he wrote an important letter to a relation, alluding to 'my regiment spoiled' in the 'Selby business' and the necessity to leave his 'few remaining men'.[47] A survey of the very comprehensive lists of prisoners taken at Selby stresses that there, of the part of the northern army left behind by Newcastle in January, a substantial part was destroyed.[48] The Yorkshire infantry, veterans of 1643, were wiped out as effective fighting formations at Selby, their officers largely captured, their cohesion gone. In York, two garrison regiments at most were left to hold the city under a Gloucestershire man who could not hope to command the gentry, whilst elements of the cavalry trickled in from Selby with reports of the disaster. The destruction of an army was the news that reached the Marquess of Newcastle on April 12th in Durham, and which brought him hurrying south to ensure possession of York, though it cost him the whole of the north in the process, apart from a few isolated garrisons. He was now a general with half an army, and that half was ruined on Marston Moor in July: had Belasyse won the battle of Selby, there would have been no siege of York and consequently, no battle of Marston Moor.

THE RELIEF OF YORK

Colonel Sir Henry Slingsby, who was to fight on Marston Moor and whose diary is an important Royalist source for the battle, had no illusions about the precarious position in which York stood after the battle of Selby. Encouraged by their success, he felt, the Parliamentarians might

> attempt some wt on ye Citty of York, having diverse wth ym inhabitance yt had forsaken their houses, & gone wth ym, & many in York yt did but faintly assist, being weari'd wth payments.[49]

Slingsby, whose regiment[50] was one of the two garrison forces, had remained in Yorkshire when the Marquess had marched north. A local man, he lived at Moor Monkton on the edge of Marston Moor, and his judgements on the course of the civil war in his county were shrewd and objective, for all his active Royalism. Of Newcastle's return to the city, he wrote

> His excellence his coming was diversly receiv'd; we in York were glad yt we had ye assistance of his army, ye foot to be put into ye Citty for ye defence of it, & ye horse to march to ye prince to enable him the better to relieve us.

Newcastle's veteran cavalry, which were to survive as a Brigade well into late 1645, and which came to be known as the Northern Horse, the name by which they are referred to here, made their way via Knaresborough down into Nottinghamshire. From there, they cut across country to join with the relieving army of Prince Rupert. Behind them, they left a city progressively encircled. Detachments of Scottish and Parliamentarian forces were set the task of mopping up minor Royalist garrisons in the county, although no attempt was made to reduce the major strongholds of Scarborough, Skipton and Pontefract, all of which had a year or more of life in them. Further north, Newcastle-upon-Tyne and Tynemouth maintained a Royalist presence, vaguely beset by a token Scottish force, while in the field remained a section of the northern Royalist army the precise strength of which is somewhat mysterious, but which could arguably have made all the difference on July 2nd had they been present.

In the midst of the tedious campaign in Durham, the Marquess of Newcastle had received a request for military aid from the Marquess of Montrose, that indisputable master of the art of surprise in warfare. Montrose, whose intention was to raise the King's standard in Scotland, put forward the plausible argument that if he could produce a successful Royalist army in his native country, it would draw back across the border a large part, if not all, of the Scottish invasion force. This was plainly irrefutable, and it is partly what was to happen eventually, although not in time to be of help to the English. Newcastle, whilst he could no doubt see the value of Montrose's plans, nevertheless had to deal with the enemy in their present condition and strength, and was not over-generous. A reliable source states that Montrose was given only 200 cavalry,[51] and perhaps two field guns, and sent on his way. The commander of the Royalists was Colonel Sir Robert Clavering.[52] Montrose's initial attempt to break into Scotland in April was foiled, but by that time Newcastle had retreated into York and the north had been abandoned to the invaders.

It is what precisely happened to Clavering's detachment that arouses curiosity. Clearly, 200 men would have made no difference either way but, as will be seen, it was argued after the battle of Marston Moor that if Prince Rupert had but waited for Clavering to join him, the increase in strength would have tipped the balance in favour of the Royalists. In fact by July 2nd Montrose was no longer with the colonel, so that Clavering was then commanding a purely English Royalist contingent. However, between April and July, Clavering's force increased significantly in strength. While the siege of York was under way, on May 10th, he and Montrose had sufficient men to advance into Northumberland and to lay siege to Morpeth Castle.[53] It is true that they acquired help from Newcastle-upon-Tyne, but even with that help, must have had something near to the 6,000 men accredited to them by the Royalist press.[54] These cannot have all been made up of Scots, for Montrose was markedly weak in forces composed of his fellow countrymen. The answer must be that Clavering's forces had increased with help from Cumbrian Royalists and also, perhaps, from units left behind in Durham when the Marquess of Newcastle made his hurried retreat into Yorkshire. The Clavering/Montrose army scored a number of small successes after their capture of Morpeth, and aroused sufficient alarm to the south to cause 1,000 Scottish horse to be detached from the siege army before York and to be sent into Durham.[55] In view of the fact that several full regiments of the Scottish army were active between Tyne and Wear anyway, that additional 1,000 must reflect the size of the Royalist force they were up against. The reinforcements for the Scottish and the failure of the Royalists to take Sunderland drove Montrose and Clavering into Newcastle-upon-Tyne. Thereafter they split up, Montrose to devote himself to his native country and Clavering to bide his time in Newcastle. The existence, however, of this substantial and undefeated Royalist force on the Tyne, was crucial to the military considerations which prompted the Marquess of Newcastle and his advisors to oppose Prince Rupert on July 1st when the latter wanted to bring the allied armies to battle.

The departure of 1,000 Scottish horse from the siege of York (it is not clear that they all returned to the siege) made little difference to the siege itself.[56] The burden of keeping in the Royalist garrison was now shared by three distinct armies: the Scots under the Earl of Leven; the Yorkshire/Lancashire forces of the Lord Fairfax; and, most importantly for events, the Eastern Association army commanded by the Earl of Manchester, whose Lt.-General of Horse was Oliver Cromwell. The siege operations were intensified, if somewhat marred by impetuosity and disagreement in the allied high command. There were several bloody skirmishes and assaults in which the Royalist garrison had the best of it, but between April and the end of June there lay a long and tedious round of duty for the opposing armies until the hopes of the defenders were raised and those of the besiegers dashed when 'he whom we so long look'd for' appeared.

The route and chronology of Rupert's march to the relief of York is set out in the contemporary Journal[57] of his marches. For much of the period which concerns this study the Prince commanded not only his own army, drawn from the south, from the Welsh borderland and from Lancashire, with some regiments of the Irish army thrown in, but also the Northern Horse and some infantry regiments which were technically under the Marquess of Newcastle's control. The Northern Horse was commanded by George Goring[58] and Sir Charles Lucas,[59] General and Lt.-General of the Horse to Newcastle respectively, and consisted of veteran regiments. In early May, before the junction of the two armies, Rupert's, pushing on towards Lancashire, was reported to consist of 2,000 horse and some 6,000 foot.[60] An advance detachment of cavalry, commanded by Colonel Sir Thomas Tyldesley,[61] drew first blood when it raided a Parliamentarian force at Garstang on May 14th. The panic which beset the Parliament's commanders in the line of Rupert's march was colossal: the correspondence which flew backwards and forwards between Manchester and London was full of anxieties, uncertainties and gross examples of self-deception as to the power of the Royalists. It was not simply that Rupert's name was one to conjure with, although that was undoubtedly important: it was also that Lancashire had been a firm recruiting ground for the Royalist armies, and although it had been overrun in 1643, it had never been entirely dominated by the committee men at Manchester and their local levies. The fear of a Lancashire rising in concert with Rupert's appearance, and the spectacle of the Northern Horse lurking in the Midlands, gave Prince Rupert decisive psychological advantages over his opponents.

On May 25th the Parliamentarian garrison of Stockport fled at the first sight of the main Royalist army, and the local commander, Colonel Alexander Rigby, took refuge in Bolton which he intended to defend.[62] Three days later, Rupert appeared before its rudimentary defences. Sir John Meldrum, who had fought at Selby in April and had then been sent into Lancashire by Lord Fairfax to observe Rupert's actions, wrote from Manchester to warn the commanders lying before York.[63] He described the way in which Royalist activism had revived, with a marked increase in the Prince's strength, and warned that unless a great army could be sent to block him at once, Lancashire and Cumbria would be overrun and nothing would stand between the allied armies before York and, as he implied, nemesis. If this was the sober judgement of a dour, professional soldier, its impact upon the high command at York siege can be appreciated. But there was nothing that could stop Rupert now. 'My hopes are', Meldrum stated,

> that this fierce thunderbolt which stikes terror among the ignorant may be easily reduced within narrow compass. If the present opportunity be neglected it will be too late to think upon anything else.

Rupert's summons to Bolton to surrender was answered by gunfire, and the town was stormed.[64] Whether or not the storm was the massacre that Parliamentarian propaganda depicted, the hard rules of war insisted that a town which defied a summons and then fell to storm was open to sack, and Rupert meant to apply those rules to the letter. 'At their entrance', one survivor recorded, 'before, behinde, to the right, and left, nothing heard but kill dead, kill dead. . . .' From Bolton, Prince Rupert swung towards Bury where, on May 30th, he joined up with the Northern Horse. Meldrum, sifting reports from scouts, estimated the Prince's total army now at 7,000 horse and 7,000 infantry, and more coming in daily to join his colours.[65] Three foot regiments from Derbyshire, those of John Frescheville,[66] John Milward[67] and Rowland Eyre[68] (the latter with some horse as well) now accompanied the Northern Horse, 'extremely barbarous' as a Parliamentarian commander, well out of the way of action, observed.[69] At York, the three generals had resolved to stay put rather than divide their armies. The relief of York was Rupert's last great flourish, and his enemies appear to have stood mesmerised. At Wigan, a town notably Royalist in attachment, the streets were strewn with flowers at his entry.

From June 7th to the 10th siege was laid to the port of Liverpool which fell to the Royalists when its govenor embarked upon a ship and put to sea. Until the 19th Rupert dallied in Lancashire, supervising new fortifications at Liverpool, commisioning a garrison regiment, and paying calls of duty upon the Countess of Derby who had maintained a Royalist presence in the county at Lathom House ever since May 1643. It has been supposed that during this period of relative inaction the Prince was toying with the idea of returning south to assist the King, who was occupied in running tactical rings around the Earl of Essex and Sir William Waller. If this was the case, by the 19th the relief of York was again uppermost in his mind.[70]

The allied army was in a serious predicament. They had failed to storm York, had indeed received setbacks in action. The Earl of Leven's caution was notorious, and as allied commander it was unlikely that he would risk a confrontation with Rupert's victorious army with the undefeated York garrison at his back. Yet nor had he contemplated detaching a part of the allied army to deal with Rupert before his power grew too great. To the Royalists marking time in Lancashire, it would have seemed that a direct march on York would produce one of two results, apart from the raising of the siege which Rupert must have felt was a foregone conclusion. It would either force an allied army, lacking in cohesion, to give battle or it would drive that army into retreat, when divisions within its command would have manifested themselves. This is almost what happened, as will be seen.

On June 24th Rupert's army was at Clitheroe Castle, and on the 26th it quartered under the walls of Skipton, a Royalist stronghold since 1642. On the 29th the Royalists entered the Fairfax family home at Denton near Otley, while the siege army before York prepared to shift to more advantageous ground to the west of the River Ouse, abandoning their entrenchments and quantities of their supplies, including guns. It looks as if Rupert's feigned approach, by way of Boroughbridge, to the west of the Ouse, lured the allies into establishing themselves on Marston Moor on June 30th expecting to have to fight and choosing to fight there. As it was, Rupert's main army kept to the east of the Ouse, and on July 1st he set his eyes upon the northern capital. Unpredictable to the last, Rupert had quite demoralised the allied commanders: the battle they had not wanted but had been willing to risk was denied them. York was relieved, and the Royalist relief army encamped in and around the city across the river. During the course of July 1st, the allied generals consulted and, although Cromwell, Sir Thomas Fairfax and David Leslie[71] may have argued against, a decision was taken to evacuate the moor and march towards Tadcaster. This decision was based on an assumption that Rupert, having elected to come to York on the east of the river, had no intention of forcing a battle. In point of fact, Rupert merely wanted to strengthen his army with the York garrison. He had every intention of bringing the allies to a fight, and towards the evening of July 1st prepared to cross the Ouse and to follow them into the flat lands of the Ainsty. Twenty-four hours would elapse, and the legend of Rupert's invicibility – amply testified to by reactions to his Lancashire march – would break. It would break because, where there had been hesitancy – in the allied command – there would be resolution, and where there had been relolution – in the Royalist command – there would appear doubts, and disobedience.

NOTES

1. The survey of events in this chapter is abstracted from a more detailed account in the writer's unpublished doctoral thesis, 'The Royalist Armies in Northern England 1642–5', University of York, 1978.
2. Sir Philip Warwick, *Memoires of the Reign of King Charles the First*, 1701, pp. 266/267.
3. Sir Thomas Glemham was a professional soldier from Suffolk, in his early 40's. Governor of York when it surrendered in July 1644 after Marston Moor was fought, he went on to become governor in turn of Carlisle and of Oxford. See Dictionary of National Biography.
4. Vicars, J., *Parliamentary Chronicles*, 1646, Vol. II, pp. 137/140.
5. Parsons, D., ed: *The Diary of Sir Henry Slingsby*, 1836, pp. 101/102.
6. Warburton, E., ed: *Memoirs of Prince Rupert and the Cavaliers*, 1849, Vol. II, p. 368.
7. Leeds City Library, Vyner Mss., 5809 T/32/50. Warburton, *op. cit.*, Vol. II, p. 370.
8. Anderson was a Newcastle-upon-Tyne merchant, knighted by the Marquess of Newcastle in 1643. See Welford, R., ed: Royalist Composition in Durham and Northumberland 1643–60, *Surtees Society*, Vol. CXI, 1905, pp. 101/105.
9. *Mercurius Aulicus*, 14.2.44, p. 820; *ibid.*, 30.1.44, p. 807.
10. Vicars, *op. cit.*, II, pp. 140/141.
11. Wood, H. M., ed: *The Registers of Whorlton, Durham*, 1908, p. 3.
12. Parsons, *Slingsby Diary, op. cit.*, p. 102.
13. *Ibid.*, p. 102. *Mercurius Aulicus*, 22.2.44, p. 844. British Library Thomason Tract, T.T. E 33 (17).
14. Langdale was a native of the East Riding of Yorkshire and, in the years before 1641, a noted opponent of the policies of the crown. A soldier of wide European experience, he became after Marston Moor, commander of the Northern Horse Brigade, became a Catholic, was raised to the peerage in 1658 by Charles II, and died after the restoration. See G.E.C., ed: *Complete Peerage*, Vol. VII, pp. 429/430.
15. Parsons, *Slingsby Diary*, p. 102 and f.n.
16. Turner, Sir James, *Memoirs of His Own Life and Times*, Edinburgh, 1839, p. 30 *et seq.*
17. For a discussion of the role of James King, created Baron Eythin in 1643 (*vide*, G.E.C., *Complete Peerage*, Vol. V, pp. 227/228) see chapter three.
18. Warburton, *op. cit.*, Vol. II, p. 381.
19. HMC, 4th report, 1879, Earl of Denbigh Mss., Vol. I, p. 264.
20. *Mercurius Aulicus*, 2.3.44, p. 859.
21. Firth, C. H., ed: *Memoirs of William Cavendish Duke of Newcastle*, 1906, pp. 34/6, 200/203.
22. Peck, F., *Desiderata Curiosa*, 1779, p. 343.
23. Terry, C. S., 'The Scottish Campaign in Northumberland and Durham', *Archaelogia Aeliana*, New Series, Vol. XXI, 1899, pp. 171/173. *Mercurius Aulicus*, 30.3.44.
24. Warburton, Vol. II, *op. cit.*, p. 397.
25. Sir John Mayney Knight and Baronet (*vide* G.E.C., *Complete Baronetage*, Vol. II, p. 93) is dealt with at some length in chapter seven.
26. Meikle, H. W., ed: Correspondence of the Scottish Commisioners in London, *Roxburgh Club*, Edinburgh 1917, p. 27.
27. Sir William Saville of Thornhill, Baronet (*vide* G.E.C., *Complete Baronetage*, Vol. I, p. 49.), a former critic of the court, was commisioned by the King in 1642.
28. Sir Francis Mackworth, knighted by Newcastle in 1643, was a career soldier from Rutlandshire, and Newcastle's Major General.

29.   For Belasyse's military career, see Moone, J., 'A Brief Relation of the Life and Memoirs of John Lord Belasyse', HMC *Ormond Mss.*, New Series, II. 1903.

30.   Firth, *Newcastle Memoirs, op. cit.*, pp. 33, 35.

31.   Moone, J., *op. cit.* Much of what follows is based upon the account given by Moone.

32.   Parsons, *Slingsby Diary*, pp. 103/104.

33.   Sir Walter Vavasour of Hazlewood, Yorkshire, Baronet (*vide* G.E.C., *Complete Baronetage*, Vol. II, p. 61) was a Catholic commissioned by Newcastle.

34.   Vicars, *op. cit.*, Vol. II, p. 154.

35.   Ibid., pp. 154, 156/157. Thomason Tract T.T. E 33 (25) *Lord Fairfax His taking of Whitby.*

36.   *For Colonel John Lambert and his later career under Cromwell's Protectorate, see Dictionary of National Biography and also Lucas Philips, C. E., Cromwell's Captains, 1938, pp. 261/397.*

37.   Hodgeson, John, 'Memoirs', *Bradford Antiquary*, New Series, Pt. XII, 1908, p. 144. Vicars, II, p. 168.

38.   Bell, R., ed: *Memoirs of the Civil War: 'Fairfax Correspondence'*, 1849, Vol. I, p. 94.

39.   For Colonel Sir Gervase Lucas, see G.E.C., *Complete Baronetage*, Vol. II, p. 226. For Porter, see Dictionary of National Biography. As Newcastle's (third) Commissary General of the Horse, his failure to respond to Belasyse's needs was even more marked.

40.   Vicars, II, pp. 168/169. Tibbutt, H. G., ed: *The Letter Books 1644–45 of Sir Samuel Luke*, 1963, p. 67. HMC 7th Report, 1879, Verney Mss., p. 477. Moone, *op. cit.*

41.   Day, W. A., ed: *The Pythouse Papers*, 1879, p. 24. Warburton, II, p. 523.

42.   Fairfax, Sir Thomas, 'Short Memoirs of the Civil War', *Yorkshire Archaeological Journal*, Vol. VIII, 1884, pp. 220/221.

43.   Sir John Meldrum was a Scottish professional soldier, and perhaps one of the best, certainly most resilient, of the commanders for the Parliament in the north. He was killed at the siege of Scarborough Castle in 1645.

44.   Henry Hastings, nicknamed 'Blind Henry Hastings' for he had the use of only one eye, was created Lord Loughborough in 1643 (*vide* G.E.C., *Complete Peerage*, VIII, pp. 166/168) and was Colonel General of Derbyshire and Nottinghamshire, which put him directly under the authority of Newcastle and of Newcastle's deputies.

45.   Parsons, *Slingsby Diary*, pp. 105/106.

46.   Wait had been Muster Master of the Yorkshire Trained Bands before the war, a professional soldier of minor gentry status. See Green, M. A. E., ed: *Calendar of the Proceedings of the Committee for Compounding*, 1889/92, & *ibid., Calendar of the Proceedings of the Committee for Advance of Money*, 1888.

47.   *Calendar of State Papers, Domestic Series*, 1644/5, pp. 197/198.

48.   Thomason Tracts, T.T. E 43 (6) *A True Relation of the Great Victory*; E 43 (14). *Lords Journals*, VI, p. 522. See also Morrell, W. W., *The History and Antiquities of Selby*, 1867, pp. 158/160 for an easily accessible transcription, occasionally in error as to precise spelling.

49.   Parsons, *Slingsby Dairy*, pp. 106/107.

50.   See Newman, P. R., 'Two York City Regiments?', *York Historian*, 2, 1978.

51.   Firth, *Newcastle Memoirs*, p. 36.

52.   Clavering was eldest son of Sir John Clavering of Callaly in Northumberland, both Catholics. He died in Westmorland in August 1644, and his regiment was drawn into the Northern Horse. See Newman, P. R., 'Catholics in Arms: The Regiment of Colonel Sir Robert Clavering of Callaly', *Northern Catholic History*, No. 9, 1979.

53.   Buchan, J., *Montrose*, 1928, p. 145.

54.   *Mercurius Aulicus*, 14.6.44, p. 1027.

55. *Calendar of State Papers, Domestic Series*, 1644, p. 241.
56. For a thorough survey of the siege of York, see that excellent work, Wenham, L. P., *The Great and Close Siege of York*, Kineton, 1970.
57. Firth, C. H., ed: 'The Journal of Prince Rupert's Marches 5 September 1642 to 4 July 1646', *English Historical Review*, Vol. 13, 1898, pp. 736/737.
58. George Goring was the eldest son of the Earl of Norwich (*vide*, G.E.C., *Complete Peerage*, IX, pp. 773/776). He ceased to command the Northern Horse after Marston Moor, where he fought well.
59. Lucas was an Essex man, younger brother of John Lord Lucas of Shenfield, and a professional soldier. One of Rupert's favourites, and an accomplished cavalry commander, he was shot to death in 1648 after the surrender of Colchester on grounds still largely unsatisfactory. See D.N.B.
60. 'Proceedings of His Majesty's Army in England under the command of His Highness Prince Rupert', *Transactions of the Royal Historical Scoiety*, New Series, Vol. XII, pp. 69/71.
61. Sir Thomas Tyldesley of Myerscough, Lancashire, fought on Marston Moor. A Catholic, commissioned in 1643, he was killed in action in 1651 at the battle of Wigan Lane.
62. Secomb, J., *History of the House of Stanley*, Preston, 1793, p. 243.
63. *Calendar of State Papers, Domestic Series* 1644, p. 176.
64. Anon, *Memorable Sieges and Battles in the North of England*, Bolton, 1786, pp. 151, 136/7; Secomb, *House of Stanley*, *op. cit.*, pp. 244/248.
65. *Calendar of State Papers, Domestic Series*, 1644.
66. John Frescheville of Staveley, Derbyshire, was elevated to the peerage in 1665 (*vide* G.E.C., *Complete Peerage*, Vol. V, pp. 578/579).
67. Colonel John Milward was of Snitterton in Derbyshire.
68. Rowland Eyre was of Hassop in Derbyshire, and a Catholic.
69. *Calendar of State Papers, Domestic Series* 1644, pp. 190/191.
70. On June 18th or 19th Prince Rupert received from his uncle a letter of crucial significance for his actions at York after the siege was raised. For a full discussion of this letter, see Chapter Three.
71. David Leslie of Pitcairly, Fifeshire, General of the Horse in the army of the Earl of Leven, was elevated to the peerage at the restoration. Critics of Cromwell have maintained that Leslie played the decisive role on Marston Moor, but that is extremely contentious.

Chapter 2

TO FIGHT OR NOT TO FIGHT

The events of June 30th – July 1st[1]

The approach of the relief army under Prince Rupert towards York obliged the allied generals to draw their forces into a body if, as his feint towards Boroughbridge indicated, it was his intention to fight his way through to the walls of the city. As it was, Rupert was conscious of his strength, less than half that of the enemy, and although he was resolved to offer battle he did not intend to do so until he had drawn upon the forces within the city. Thus the allied army, not entirely committed to the idea of battle anyway, was given twenty-fours hours breathing space, sufficient time for doubts and uncertainties to present themselves again. Sir Thomas Fairfax, one of the younger and more resolute commanders, remembered 'We were divided in o^r opinions w^t to doe. The English were for fighting,' he observed wryly, 'the Scotts for Retreating, to gaine (as they alledged) both time and place of Advantage'. The Earl of Leven, whose caution has already been remarked on, while he could not have avoided battle had Rupert forced it upon him on June 30th, certainly had no desire to court possible disaster by waiting for Rupert's victorious army to join up with the undefeated forces within York. Considering the fact that Leven and his colleagues must have been aware of the size of the two Royalist armies, this unwillingness to engage is both a tribute to Prince Rupert and a reproach to the allied high command. Even had it been true, as Stockdale recorded, that on Friday June 28th the allies believed that Rupert had effected a junction with Sir Robert Clavering and his forces, the numerical advantage still lay with the allies, and significantly so.

THE OPPOSING FORCES

The strengths of the opposing armies on Marston Moor are no longer a matter of historical dispute. C. H. Firth and, latterly and conclusively,

Peter Young, in his monograph, have extrapolated the necessary details to arrive at a very fair estimate. The Scottish army, the largest of the three, was weakest in cavalry, perhaps 2,000 in all, while the Fairfax army had an equivalent number of horse, but their 2,000 represented perhaps half of the total army under Lord Fairfax's command following Meldrum's detachment to Manchester. The bulk of the allied cavalry belonged to the Earl of Manchester, 4,000 in all, which gave the allies 8,000 horse to deploy. These varied in quality. Scottish cavalry had not shown themselves very able during the northern campaign, but their general's unwillingness to commit them must be taken into account. Lord Fairfax had veteran Yorkshire regiments, but also forces drawn from the decidedly inexperienced Lancashire levies, the type of soldiery that had melted away before Rupert's advance. The true quality of the allied cavalry lay in the Earl of Manchester's regiments, under the strong hand of Oliver Cromwell, who had learned a hard lesson about cavalry at Edgehill in 1642. It was no accident that when battle came to be prepared for the Scottish horse were deployed as support for the two English cavalry forces, David Leslie to support Cromwell, and the Earl of Eglinton to support Thomas Fairfax.

The bulk of the Scottish army consisted in foot, perhaps 13,500 in all, but again of variable quality. Leven's reluctance to commit them to battle immediately after the invasion had begun, and Sir James Turner's telling observations, will be remembered. Even so, given proper direction and resolution, the sheer bulk of that infantry could prove a telling factor in battle. Lord Fairfax might deploy between 2,000 to 3,000 infantry, again of mixed quality, whilst the army of the Eastern Association could field 4,000 infantry. Young has reckoned the total allied strength at 28,000 men, a truly enormous army for the civil war period, but its inherent weakness lay in its mixture of veterans and raw units and, as has been seen, in the hesitancies of its high command. Further, the jealous concern which Leven, Lord Fairfax and Manchester showed for their own armies, meant that when battle was eventually joined, the vast bulk of the allied cavalry – those under Cromwell – were to be deployed on one part of the battlefield, leaving Sir Thomas Fairfax and Eglinton with perhaps only 3,000 horse on the allied right wing. But this is to anticipate events. The point is that when the allied generals disputed about what to do, they had, and they knew that they had, numerical advantage. If it is true that Thomas Fairfax and

Cromwell did not share the hesitancy of their superiors, it was because they did not share the mesmerised response to the presence of Rupert across the River Ouse.

Meldrum in Manchester had sent despatches to London and to York reporting on Rupert's movements and recounting estimates of his strength. When, in late June, the Prince crossed into Yorkshire, his army was probably 14,000 strong, roughly half-and-half cavalry and infantry. Like the army of Lord Fairfax, this was a mixed body: at its best it consisted of some of Rupert's veteran cavalry regiments from the Oxford army reinforced on the Welsh border by units that had passed from Arthur Lord Capel to John Lord Byron, the latter commanding these border troops which were largely drawn from Lancashire and the borderland. Although these cavalry regiments were experienced, the best at Rupert's disposal were the regiments of the Northern Horse under Goring. The *Proceedings of His Majesty's Army* reckoned the Northern Horse 5,000 strong on May 30th, although two reports of enemy observers on that date[2] estimated them at 2,000 or 3,000 in all. In Chapter One it was pointed out that when Newcastle went north on January 28th he took with him 3,000 horse, which were subsequently reinforced by a further 1,000 under Lucas, while perhaps a further 1,000 had come in from Cumbria. If wastage had been minimal or had been made up elsewhere – perhaps when the Northern Horse were at large after the siege of York had begun – this would square with the 5,000 reported by *Proceedings*. However, while it is true that Newcastle retained at least one cavalry regiment in York with him, that of Colonel Sir Marmaduke Langdale,[3] we cannot assume that losses in manpower in Durham were necessarily repaired. It might be a safer estimate to reckon the Northern Horse at 4,000 at most, since we also cannot account for the reputed strength of the Clavering forces which included northern cavalry regiments.

Clearly, an allied move to obstruct an army of 14,000 men with 28,000 on June 30th would have recommended itself even to the Earl of Leven, however much he might then balk at the prospect of that 14,000 united with the York garrison. But it is the question of the strength of the York garrison that is perplexing. Newcastle, as well as his cavalry, had gone into Durham with 5,000 foot, and had there raised further regiments and received reinforcement from Cumbria. Allowing for wastage in infantry units, always more marked than in cavalry, and given the weather conditions and the speed of the retreat to York in April, it is improbable that he got back into the city with more than 4,000 veteran foot intact. John Belasyse at Selby on April 11th had deployed perhaps 5,000 foot and 1,500 horse – these latter, Mackworth's Brigade – and, as has been argued, lost the larger part of them. A reliable source[4] estimated that at Selby 1,000 Royalists were killed and wounded and no fewer than 1,800 taken prisoner. A large number of officers were also taken, which would be instrumental in the break up of such recognisable regiments as may have escaped the slaughter: the despair occasioned by Selby is present in the attitude of Sir Walter Vavasour, and although it cannot now be quantified, the impact of the defeat, of Belasyse's capture, and of the pressure away to the north would undermine whatever morale remained. We must suppose that if any units escaped from Selby and made their way into York these would have been chiefly Mackworth's Horse and a few companies of foot. Given the presence of two garrison regiments which remained permanently in the city, both when Selby was fought and at Marston Moor, the total stength of the Marquess of Newcastle's York garrison on July 1st was probably 5,000 foot and up to 2,000 horse. If all these joined together and acted in unison with Rupert, it gave him an army of 21,000, still numerically inferior but not alarmingly so. That the York forces did not act in full unison with the relief army depleted the Royalist forces on Marston Moor by perhaps 3,000 or more, a point to which we shall return. Leven, of course, could not anticipate that there would not be a full conjunction.

TO FIGHT OR NOT TO FIGHT

From Stockdale we learn that the Earl of Leven and Lord Fairfax, neither of whom wanted to risk battle, were under pressure from their immediate subordinates to fight anyway. Leven could argue that they ought to wait until promised help from the west arrived, consisting of an army under the command of Meldrum and the Earl of Denbigh which was expected to appear near Wakefield on Wednesday, July 3rd. This information came to hand on June 30th, the day on which Rupert appeared at Knaresborough and on which the siege was raised and the allied army withdrew to the moorlands to block his advance. When Rupert avoided that confrontation, Leven could dismiss the immediate necessity of battle, and stress the value of a link with Meldrum and Denbigh before attempting it. Throughout Monday July 1st the allied commanders argued and dithered.

The euphoria at Rupert's appearance before York was rapidly and unpleasantly dispelled. Some 2,000 of his cavalry, according to Cholmeley, carried away by their success, got into the town to fraternise with the garrison; these cavalry were probably northern elements from Newcastle's army. It is also likely that Colonel Sir John Mayney gained entrance with them, perhaps even sent by Rupert to deliver an unprepossessing message. 'The prince', noted Slingsby, who was in York, 'sends in to my L^d of Newcastle to meet him wth those forces he had in York'. The *Rupert Diary*, based on information supplied by Colonel Sir Francis Cobbe, commander of Cliffords Tower during the siege, states: 'ye P sent to ye Earle [*sic*] of Newcastle to signify to him that he had ordr to fight ye Enemy'. It was true that Prince Rupert possessed 'a supreme commission above the Marquess' (Cholmeley) but even so this was not quite the way one commander presented himself to another, and it is understandable that the York commanders who had endured so much took a fit of pique at this offhand manner. The Duchess of Newcastle recorded later: 'My Lord immediately sent some persons of quality to attend his Highness, and to invite him into the city to consult. . . .' Whether or not Rupert did enter York is largely irrelevant, but that some meeting took place is apparent.

Precisely who attended that meeting is unknown, but apart from Rupert and Newcastle, James King, Baron Eythin must have been there. Eythin was cautious, and not the best of men to have as an advisor at this time, particularly since his dislike of Rupert was widely known and cannot have been concealed. They were to clash again within an hour of the battle of Marston Moor being joined. For the present however Eythin was concerned only to reinforce Newcastle's doubts. The Marquess explained to Rupert that it would take some time to open a gate to permit his forces to leave properly (all the gates of York had been blocked with earth and masonry at the start of the siege), in this case Micklegate for reasons which will be explained. That this was partly employed to gain time is implicit in the Duchess of Newcastle's account, which she took down at her husband's later direction. 'After some conferences, the Marquess declared his mind to the Prince, desiring his Highness not to attempt anything as yet upon the enemy; for he had intelligence that there was some discontent between them, and that they were resolved to divide themselves.' If the prospect of division in the allied army was an assumption, it was based upon accurate knowledge of the disputes in the allied command. Rupert was not impressed, whereupon 'besides my Lord expected within two days Colonel Clavering with above three thousand men out of the North, and two thousand drawn out of several garrisons'. Clavering's strength has been discussed, and if this was a true indication of numbers, which there is no reason to suppose it was not, there might have been good grounds for waiting. Curiously, this increase in strength anticipated on July 3rd bears striking resemblance to Leven's anticipation of Meldrum and Denbigh's arrival with a force of unspecified size at Wakefield.

There is a lot that we do not know about the nature of military intelligence at the time: did Leven, for example, know of Clavering's approach? Did Rupert have warning of the movement by Meldrum and Denbigh? Or did Rupert on his part, and Cromwell and Thomas Fairfax on their part, prefer present reality to future possibilities? Other arguments were presented, according to Cholmeley, who reiterated the Clavering aspect. Rupert 'came into the country with such dread . . . he might not only have increased his own army, but surely the enemy would have diminished', a flattering approach which likewise failed to elicit any response from Rupert beyond a flat affirmation that he intended to fight. At this juncture in the conference, Rupert stated that 'hee was obliged not to let the enemy march too far out of his reach, having a command from the King to fight the Scottish army whereso'er he met them'. Cholmeley's observation is supported by the Duchess: 'his Highness answered my Lord that he had a letter from his Majesty . . . with a positive and absolute command to fight the enemy; which in obedience . . . he was bound to perform'. So crucial has this 'letter' been to historians of the battle of Marston Moor, that it is strange a full assessment of it has never been attempted.

On June 11th the King had written to Rupert urging him to march on into Yorkshire.[5] On the 14th he sent a further letter, which has been cited by all writers as *the* letter to which Rupert alluded in conference on July 1st.

> Nepueu. first I must congratulat with you, for your good successes, asseuring you that the things themselfes ar no more welcome to me, than that you are the means: I know the importance of the supplying you with

powder for which I have taken all possible wais, having sent both to Ireland and Bristow, as from Oxford this bearer is well satisfied, that it is impossible to have at present, but if he tell you that I may spare them hence, I leave you to judge, having but 36 left; but what I can gett from Bristow (of wch there is not much certaintie, it being threatened to be beseiged) you shall have But now I must give you the trew stat of my Affaires, wch if their condition be such as enforses me to give you more peremptory comands than I would willingly doe, you must not take it ill. If Yorke be lost, I shall esteeme my Crown little lesse, unlesse supported by your suddaine Marche to me, & a Miraculious Conquest in the South, before the effects of the Northern power can be found heere; but if Yorke be relived, & you beate the Rebelles Armies of both Kingdoms, which ar before it, then but otherwise not, I may possiblie make a shift, (upon the defensive) to spinn out tyme, untill you come to assist mee: Wherefor I comand and conjure you, by the dewty & affection which I know you beare me, that (all new enterpryses laid aside) with all your force to the relife of Yorke; but if that be eather lost, or have fried themselves from the besiegers, or that for want of pouder you cannot undertake that worke; that you immediatly March, with your whole strength, to Woster, to assist me & my Army, without whiche, or your having relived Yorke by beating the Scots, all the successes you can afterwards have, most infallibly, will be uselesse unto me. . . .

Although Rupert never showed any letter to Newcastle, we will assume that this was indeed the letter referred to by Cholmeley and the Duchess and that it was probably the letter which made Rupert resolve to march towards York on June 19th. But what does the letter actually say? A close reading of the letter can allow us to dismiss right away the canard that Digby, the King's adviser, wrote the letter himself to force Rupert to fight. Peter Young has judiciously observed: 'A modern staff officer would be hard pressed indeed to make of this a direct order to fight a battle after York had been relieved.' Quite so. The letter is less a letter of instruction than one of information, news and advice, confirming that what Rupert had marched north to achieve was still, in the King's opinion, worth attempting. Examining the letter more closely, and stripping away the mythology which has grown around it, it cannot be argued that the King equated the loss of York with the loss of the war itself, therefore it cannot be argued that this letter was a summary command to relieve York whatever the cost. Indeed, in alluding to Rupert's want of powder, the King provided his nephew with an escape clause, and hints at an exchange of letters between the two of them during May and June, none of which have survived. Leaving aside the usual formalities of a royal letter, the 'comand and conjure you', we have a letter written by a man whose style and meaning would have been clear to Rupert, who had received innumerable such despatches, and which offered him an excuse to abandon the York march on sound military grounds. Had the King truly placed supreme emphasis upon relieving York, he would have moved heaven and earth to let his nephew have the means to perform it. The letter permitted Rupert to act upon his own initiative in the light of accumulated intelligence from the south.

If Rupert did receive an order to fight come what may, he did not receive it in the letter of the 14th which was emphatically not such an order. Is it possible that Prince Rupert, confident of his own abilities, and in danger of being thwarted by Newcastle and his advisers, played an ace he did not actually have either up his sleeve or in his pocket? Creating, in the wake of defeat on Marston Moor, a myth which his reputation needed? For Newcastle to actually demand to see such a letter, in view of Rupert's superior authority, would have been gross discourtesy and gross insubordination. Time was slipping away, and time was of the essence. Rupert presented the Marquess with a *fait accompli*.

The Duchess recorded that when Rupert stated that he had an order to fight, and would do so immediately, before the opportunity slipped away, the Marquess replied, 'That he was ready and willing, for his part, to obey his Highness in all things'. Leaving orders that the entire Royalist army be ready to march at four in the morning of Tuesday July 2nd, Rupert and the York commanders parted company, the Marquess returning into the city.

What happened next, in York, is significant for the outcome of the battle of Marston Moor. 'Several of my Lord's friends advised him not to engage in battle', wrote the Duchess. 'It is considered', Cholmeley wrote, 'those which had relation to the Marquess his army did not in their affections so harmoniously comply to this great work as was requisite.' Sir Francis Cobbe stated clearly that James King, Baron Eythin told the Marquess not to commit all his garrison forces to so dangerous an enterprise. Eythin was not by any means contented with his position, indeed, in April he had even wanted to resign his commission and go into Europe[6] and he pressed Newcastle hard, pointing out the affront to his dignity which Rupert had, he alleged, delivered.

41

Nevertheless, the Marquess, whose concept of loyalty to the King had required him to overcome reaction both to Rupert's manner towards him and insistence that he knew best, 'answered . . . that happen what would, he would not shun to fight, for he had no other ambition to live and die a loyal subject to his Majesty'. If this was posturing to conceal wounded pride it did not matter. Newcastle had every intention of obeying Rupert. It was a pity that he could not communicate this necessity to Eythin.

RUPERT MOVES FROM YORK

Rupert's forces had seized a bridge of boats across the River Ouse, and the Prince now prepared to move his army across to the other bank. In York, Micklegate bar was unblocked to facilitate the movement of the garrison foot to comply with the Prince's instructions. From Micklegate bar, a 'pack and prime way' led directly across country to the village of Hessay and so on to the moorlands beyond. Along this route the York foot would take the most direct way to the battlefield, while no doubt Mackworth's cavalry would rapidly join forces with the Northern Horse in Rupert's army. From Micklegate, in the dawn of Tuesday July 2nd, the Marquess of Newcastle emerged in his coach, intending his infantry to be mustered by Eythin and to follow behind. Morning broke, and lengthened towards afternoon before Eythin himself and the infantry emerged. The delay, whether or not it was avoidable, contributed to the defeat of the Royalist army.

Beyond attempts to dissuade Newcastle from fighting, or at least from committing all his forces to Rupert's plan, what passed in York after the conference with Rupert and before noon on July 2nd is a matter of some dispute. What is beyond dispute is that the York foot arrived on the battlefield at some time between 2:00 and 4:00 in the afternoon long after Newcastle himself appeared, and too late to enable Rupert to take advantage of some confusion in the allied army. Cholmeley stated that when Newcastle came to the moor, he told Prince Rupert that 'his foot had been a plundering in the enemy's trenches and that it was impossible to have got them together at the time prefixed, but that he had left General King about the worke, who would bring them up with all expedition that might be'. It is quite probable that after months of confinement, the garrison had taken advantage of the hurried flight of the allies to scavenge in their lines. But they had had all day on July 1st to do it, and if they were veteran regiments, there is no reason why Eythin could not have brought them into order, even if he had some men missing, by 4:00 a.m. on the 2nd. By leaving Eythin behind him to see to the mustering of the foot, Newcastle also left behind him the man who was reluctant to commit the entire strength of the infantry to battle. Perhaps he hoped by delay to force Rupert to abandon the whole idea: and when it was apparent this would not succeed, he took with him to the field a portion of the Royalist garrison. Eythin's entire role in the preliminaries to the battle was equivocal.

Further evidence for the late arrival of the York infantry on the battlefield is to be found in the order of battle drawn up by Sir Bernard de Gomme on Marston Moor itself. This plan is an accurate and detailed guide to the Royalist dispositions, but with one major exception: the York foot are lumped together into seven blocks. This marked absence of detail indicates that de Gomme showed the York foot where they were *intended* to be deployed rather than an actual alignment. This may well be the paper of which Eythin said, when shown it upon his arrival in the afternoon, 'By God . . . it is very fine on the paper, but there is no such thing in the field.' Writers have supposed this to mean that the royalist dispositions were badly made, whereas Eythin may well have meant that the reality of his late arrival rendered the plan itself invalid unless he could rapidly deploy his infantry in accordance with it. As will be shown, the attempt to do this occasioned the Allied advance. Cholmeley who, as has been said, was in a very good position to know what had happened, recorded that Prince Rupert 'seeing the . . . foot were not come up, would with his own foot have been falling upon the enemy', but he was deterred from this by Newcastle, 'telling him he had 4,000 good foot as were in the world' and, by four o'clock in the afternoon of July 2nd, Eythin arrived with 'not above 3,000'. There seems to be little doubt that upon his appearance Eythin was required to move his regiments into the positions stipulated by Rupert and worked out on paper by de Gomme, and when asked what he thought of the deployment, told Rupert 'he did not approve it being drawn too near the enemy, and in a place of disadvantage'. Rupert suggested that the army might be pulled back a distance, to which Eythin made the accurate reply: 'No sir . . . it is too late.'

43

The evidence for the nature of de Gomme's plan is strengthened by a curious anomaly, in that while all sources refer to 25 guns captured from the Royalists during the battle and recovered afterwards on July 3rd and 4th, de Gomme expressly cites only 16 pieces of ordinance. It looks as if these 16 were the guns conveyed by Rupert from Lancashire, perhaps augmented by enemy cannon picked up in the trenches around York. The other nine guns can only have been carried from York with the York infantry, and if de Gomme had had these on the moor when he drew his plan, his record would then have tallied with the reports of captured ordnance.

There is also the omission of Colonel Sir John Mayney from the battle plan, who was a Brigade commander in the Northern Horse, and Colonel Sir Marmaduke Langdale. Peter Young, in his revision of the plan, inserted Langdale but did not know of the evidence for Mayney's presence. Langdale was a cavalry commander who remained in York with Newcastle during the siege, evidenced by the presence there of his regiment. Mayney, it has been suggested, went into York on July 1st perhaps conveying Rupert's summons to combine the two armies, for he had been Newcastle's last messenger to the Prince before the siege of York. It seems under the circumstances to be likely that neither Langdale or Mayney were included in the plan because they had not arrived, and the dispositions of the Northern Horse on the Royalist left wing reflected the distribution of commands prevailing upon the morning of July 2nd. Langdale was superior to the other named commanders, with the exception of Goring and Lucas, and would have assumed a command upon arrival. The omissions of Langdale, Mayney, the York foot commanders, and a further nine guns strongly supports the contention that de Gomme's plan was drawn at a relatively early stage of deployment. Its claim to accuracy lies mainly in the depiction of the Royalist right wing and the infantry of the centre, forces which were with Rupert on the moor in the morning, and to a certain extent the deployment of the Northern Horse on the left wing.

A further anomaly of the de Gomme plan is that while Rupert's Lifeguard of Horse were drawn up in position by de Gomme, Newcastle's Lifeguard is missing. Cholmeley states that when the Marquess left York 'about 9 a clock' in the morning of July 2nd, he was 'accompanied by all the gentlemen of quality which were in York who cast themselves into a troop commanded by Sir Thomas Mettam'[7] who was killed in the battle. This troop no doubt included Colonel Sir Henry Slingsby, whose own infantry regiment remained in York. If we accept that the term 'troop' here denotes a flexible unit numerically speaking, it could, and probably did, consist of a 100 or more gentlemen, and the presence of so distinguished a troop on the moor would have been recorded by de Gomme if the plan had not already been drafted.

On July 1st the decision to fight or not to fight for the Royalists was made by Rupert, assented to by Newcastle, and grudgingly accepted by Eythin. It was not until the morning of July 2nd that the allied generals were obliged to make a similar decision to fight. Events turned upon what Rupert would choose to do, and the battle turned upon what Lord Eythin failed to do.

NOTES

1. Henceforth, unless indicated by the appropriate footnote, all sources cited will be found set out in the bibliography of sources for the battle.
2. *Calendar of State Papers, Domestic Series* 1644, pp. 188, 190/191.
3. Parsons, *Slingsby Diary*, p. 111.
4. HMC 7th Report 1879, Verney Mss., p. 447.
5. Warburton, I, p. 518.
6. Green, M. A. E., ed: *Letters of Queen Henrietta Maria*, 1857, p. 238.
7. Sir Thomas Metham of Metham had commanded an infantry regiment in 1642 but this had been disbanded after it had melted away before the walls of Hull in that year. Metham was in his 67th year when he was killed on Marston Moor.

Chapter 3

PRELUDE TO BATTLE

The events on Marston Moor between 9:00 am and 4:00 pm, Tuesday July 2nd 1644

THE BATTLEFIELD IN 1644

The highest point of the ridge, lying to the south of the battlefield of Marston Moor, gives a commanding view of the whole and is marked now by a group of trees known traditionally as Cromwell's Clump. The trees are on the 38m contour line, and the battlefield, spread out before them, descends over a distance of roughly 1,575 yards to the 15m contour. Initially, this descent is very sharp, virtually 1 in 8, a drop from the Clump itself down to the 30m contour in a matter of 75 yards, and then a more progressive descent from this latter line to the 23m contour takes place over a distance of 300 yards. It was on this 23m line that, more or less, the front of the allied army was drawn up between 9:00 am and 2:00 pm on July 2nd. Thereafter, the descent becomes barely perceptible, reaching the 15m contour over a distance of 1,200 yards, and the bulk of the Royalist army was to be drawn up on that gradual slope facing the allies. Before the onset of battle, the rival front lines were to be not less than a quarter of a mile, and rarely more than half a mile, apart, with a forward line of Royalist musketeers drawn closer to the allied front.

Legend asserts that at the point where the trees of the Clump dominate the skyline, the allied generals, Leven, Lord Fairfax and the Earl of Manchester, established their command post around noon. On a clear day the observer at that point could see away to the north-east the walls of York Minster and, many miles northwards, the line of the Hambleton Hills. Of more immediate concern to the three generals would have been the advantageous command which the position gave of everything transpiring in the Royalist army beneath them. It was on this ridge line, and perhaps in the vicinity of the Clump, that Thomas

46

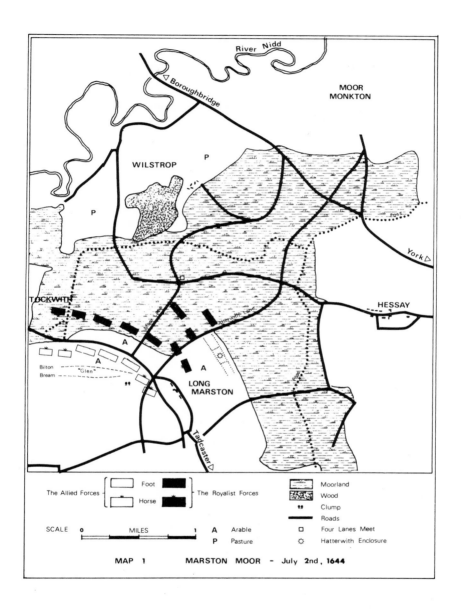

MAP 1   MARSTON MOOR – July 2nd, 1644

Fairfax, Cromwell and Leslie stood at 9:00 am to watch the Royalists spreading onto the moorland from the direction of York.

In 1644 the ridge was, as it now is, cultivated land, not part of the open fields of the village of Long Marston, but brought in piecemeal from the waste over the course of centuries. Known as Marston Fields, they stretched from the westernmost edge of the village away west towards the Bilton Bream, which was to mark the extreme left flank of the allied battle formations. The steep slope down from the Clump was under crop – wheat or rye – as was all the light, sandy soil of the slope down into the glen, and so up to the 23m contour, stopping only at the edge of the old trackway which connected the villages of Long Marston and Tockwith. This track lay roughly a third of a mile from the Clump due north, while the first buildings of Marston village lay about half a mile to the north-east. Further on still could be seen the roofs of Hessay. The taking in of the waste had extended to the north beyond the Long Marston/Tockwith road, where the soil had the same light, easily worked qualities as that found south of the road. After about 300 yards however this light, tilled soil was transformed into heavy, wet clay, and from that point onwards the moorland proper began.

The allied commanders were familiar with the terrain. They had been encamped upon it all day on July 1st, debating what to do. It was an area of scrub grass, gorse and bracken, spread with thorn, and with areas of bog indicated by rich, dank vegetation, survivals of which remain to this day. Narrow tracks criss-crossed it, made up of tons of cobbles in which fragments of 14th and 15th century pottery, still to be found, were scattered. These tracks facilitated the driving of beasts onto the open common moorland for grazing, but it is unlikely that any cultivation had so far been attempted on very unpromising land. There may have been pockets of arable lying between the Four Lanes Meet and Wilstrop Wood, but these may have been relics of the encroachment on the waste of the villagers of Wilstrop, which had been thrown down at the end of the 15th century by an enclosing landowner.[1] The wood itself has been vigorously replanted and cut back in acreage, but from the evidence of the older part appears to have been thinly planted with trees, many of these substantial oaks and elms. Relics of the older woodland can be seen in the post-enclosure hedgerows adjacent to the wood. Around the wood were acres of open parkland, created early in the 16th century, but with a fair scattering of cottages, particularly to the

48

east of the wood and under its immediate edge.

Access onto the moorland from York could be had by any one of three routes. The northernmost of these was the road to Boroughbridge, established as a turnpike in the early 18th century, but certainly in existence and based upon an older, Roman, way, in 1644. It was along this road that Prince Rupert's army, having crossed the Ouse by the bridge of boats at Poppleton, made its way to the battlefield, probably leaving the road and cutting across the open fields of Hessay north of that village. The most immediate route however lay from Micklegate Bar across country into Hessay itself, and this route would have been taken by the York infantry during the course of July 2nd.[2] A 'pack and prime way', laid down alongside an existing road, but built up with stones and maintained in good repair for the easy passage of pack trains bearing wool and other commodities, it offered a firm means of access at all seasons of the year when other roads might be here and there awash, or sunk in thick mud. Once this route entered the township of Hessay, it diverged, running north and south of the village, meeting again just to the west and running on more or less directly towards the moorland, bridging the ancient Foss Dyke and meeting the tracks which traversed the moorland itself. The third route from York, by no means so direct, was that of the modern Wetherby road, passing through Acomb, and turning away from the village of Long Marston towards Hutton Wandesley, from which Long Marston had itself grown. Some detachments of allied troops from the siege may well have travelled along this third route on June 30th, and branched off for the general rendezvous on the moor, passing through Long Marston itself.

Apart from the narrow, cobbled ways which traversed parts of the moorland and which had been laid down on severely utilitarian principles, there were two more important tracks. The seventeenth-century observer, standing on the site of the Clump, and turning to his right, would see the ridge shelving gradually down to a track coming up from the south, from the direction of the Wetherby road, crossing the shoulder of the ridge at a point known locally as Cromwell's Gap, and running on to join the Long Marston/Tockwith road at a point approximately 200 yards to the west of the westernmost building in Long Marston. Crossing this east-west route, the track, now known as the Atterwith or Hatterwith Lane, traversed the cultivated land, from which it was demarcated by a ditch and perhaps a hedge running parallel

49

with it, and issued onto the moorland proper. The Atterwith Lane branched off northwards and so ran on to join the Boroughbridge road, meeting on its way the track from Hessay which was the extension of the 'pack and prime way' from Micklegate. About half way along the Atterwith Lane, on its right, where since enclosure, the Fox Covert, a game preserve, has stood, were two or three enclosures brought in from the waste in the late 16th century by the Thwaites, lords of the manor of Long Marston, and known as the Hatterwith enclosures.[3] They formed a barrier between the open fields of Long Marston and the spread of moorland to their north-east.

The other important track across the moorland was Sandy Lane or Moor Lane, alternatively known as 'Bloody Lane' thanks to the extravagances of 19th century antiquarians. Changes in land use since enclosure in 1766, while not obliterating the track itself, have deprived it of its immediate importance. In 1644, after half a mile or so, it split into three at a junction known as Four Lanes Meet. It was at Four Lanes Meet that, in 1654, during a Royalist plot to seize the city of York, local Royalist gentlemen made their rendezvous only to be dispersed by certain information that their plans were known to the authorities in the city. Their route to the city would therefore have been along the metalled track through Hessay and so to Micklegate. This was the eastern branch of the Moor Lane which was finally destroyed in the early part of the 20th century. The northern branch ran towards Wilstrop Wood, swung sharply east away from the wood, eventually joining the Boroughbridge road. The third branch of the track turned due west, and then swung north-west towards the River Nidd, skirting Wilstrop Wood on its right. In 1644 all of these tracks, if not thronged with travellers, were frequented and essential to communications in an area of bog and moor.

Writers on the battle have insisted upon inserting on their plans a third lane, at the eastern edge of Tockwith village, Kendal Lane. This lane post-dates the battle of Marston Moor by roughly 150 years, being laid down by the enclosure commissioners during Tockwith's enclosure at the end of the 18th century. It is therefore erroneous to write of the Royalist right wing being anchored on Kendal Lane. The Royalist right wing was not anchored at all, which was half its problem.

These major features would be noted by the allied soldier, commander or commanded, established on the ridge and waiting for battle to begin, but they would be less apparent to the Royalist marching into line on the flat moorland with no opportunity to take in his entire surroundings. He would see the ranks of his comrades, the colours rising above the heads of infantry and cavalry alike and, to the south, the masses of the allied army on the elevated ground. Those who recorded their impressions of the battle, when they alluded to terrain features at all, naturally remembered those which had been either obstacles or aids to the fulfilment of their role or duty, although some did remark upon general features. Between the array of the Royalist army and the allied forces shown as established on the ridge, de Gomme drew a line curving away from the allies and running the length of the Royalist front, beneath which his notation reads 'These hedge was Lined with musquetiers'. What this does tell us is that Prince Rupert pushed a skirmishing line of musketeers forward of his main army either to harass the allies as they drew into formation, or, more probably, to disrupt any advance by the enemy before the Royalists could be drawn into battle order in keeping with the ideas sketched in the plan. Some writers have, on the evidence of the plan, accepted that a hedge did indeed lie between the two armies in a virtually unbroken line, serving as an obstacle to the allies. Others, present on the field, who mentioned this 'obstacle' are at variance with de Gomme.

The curve of the hedge on the plan resembles closely the line between cultivated land immediately north of the Long Marston/Tockwith road, and the expanse of moorland on which the Royalist forces were deployed. However, the assumption that this cultivated land, taken in piecemeal over many generations, possessed a single such barrier of uniform density and type, is inherently improbable. De Gomme was merely indicating a line, not indulging in any precision as to its component parts. Simeon Ashe noted, from the ridge, 'the hedge and ditch betwixt themselves and us', whilst Captain Stewart, on the allied right wing, wrote of 'a great ditch between the Enemy and us, which ran along the front of the Battell, only between the Earl of Manchester's foot and the enemy there was a plain'. Stewart's account of terrain features on the right of the allied line is crucially important, and must be returned to. Lionel Watson, the allied Scoutmaster General, noted only 'a small ditch and a bank betwixt us and the Moor'. Lumsden referred to 'ane ditch which they [the Royalists] had in possession'. Clearly, some form of obstacle existed but that it bore any relation to de Gomme's unbroken, curving hedgeline is equally as clearly not the case. Stewart particularly noted that no obstacle at all lay between the infantry of the Earl of Manchester on the left of the allied centre, and the Royalist infantry opposed to them. What this all points to is that the ditch and bank were one and the same thing, and ran between Moor Lane and the Atterwith Lane, dividing the cultivated land from the moorland. There may, at one point, have been a hedge. The cavalry of the allied right wing, and the infantry of the right of the allied centre, crossing this cultivated land into action, were confronted by the bank. More pronounced at the Atterwith Lane end, the cultivated land gave out in a steep bank (now levelled) which stood well above the height of a man. Allied forces traversing the arable would, therefore, find themselves dropping, as if into a ditch, perhaps six feet onto the level of the moorland, an obstacle sufficient to impede orderly deployment and even to create consternation and panic. While it is true that from their sojourn on the moor on July 1st the allied commanders would have been aware of this obstacle, that would not have precluded them from having to negotiate it. In a sense Thomas Fairfax was fortunate in that he could send his cavalry down the Atterwith Lane which, on its old course, cut through the obstacle and rendered it no hazard at all, but his difficulty then was in debouching from the lane onto the moorland in the face of Royalist musketry concentrated against this weakness in the defence. As will be seen, the slaughter at this point was enormous and may have accounted for a good half to two-thirds of all allied casualties. This hazard would correspond both with the bank, described by Watson, and the ditch, in the sense of an apparent depression, alluded to by Stewart.

Running west from Moor Lane as if in continuation of this line and marking the point at which cultivated and waste land met, was a small ditch perhaps with a hedge parallel to it, probably on the north side. It is significant that Colonel Sir Henry Slingsby, a local man who must have known the moorland fairly well, wrote of 'ye hedges of ye Cornfeilds' rather than of a single hedge, and his remark implies a lack of a uniform barrier of any kind. This westward ditch and hedge terminated after about 150 yards and then the cultivated land and the moorland converged on Stewart's 'plain'.

Reverting to the terrain of the allied right, the Atterwith Lane area, Stewart wrote of Sir Thomas Fairfax's cavalry having 'no passage but at a narrow lane . . . upon the one side . . . was a Ditch, and on the other an Hedge'. This was the (now vanished) continuation of the track crossing the ridge from the south and leading up towards the Hatterwith Enclosures. Sir Thomas Fairfax, when dealing with his less successful enterprises was, to say the least, sparing in his descriptions, but noted on this wing the 'whins and ditches which we were to pass over before we could get to the Enemy', while Bowles, admittedly a primary/secondary source, wrote of 'the worst part of the ground, being so full of whinnes that his horse could not march up, and was next the hedges possessed by the enemy'. While the account of what befell the allied right wing is best dealt with elsewhere, such sources as mention terrain on the east of the battlefield concur in saying that Thomas Fairfax was beset by severe handicaps in the deployment of his cavalry, handicaps emphasised by Royalist dispositions that made the more leisurely negotiation of the only track hazardous in the extreme.[4]

Another major point of interest lies in the nature of the ground over which Cromwell and the allied left wing of cavalry charged to the attack. Lionel Watson, writing of the allied position in general terms, observed 'we were put to draw our men into a Corne-field close to the Moore, making way by our Pioneers to get ground to extend the wings of our army to such a distance, that wee might conveniently fight'. Doubtless the troops also amused themselves in flattening the corn, the height of which, according to Ashe, 'prov'd no small inconvenience'. The employment of pioneers is, however, important, and probably occurred on the allied left, since the allied right was more or less anchored, 'being placed just by Merston Town side, the town on our right hand, fronting on the east'. In this context, town should be taken as including garths and enclosures immediately adjacent to the village, and not buildings as such. Cromwell and the left wing, however, extended towards Tockwith and took possession of the Bilton Bream with its coney or rabbit warren. These warrens were not small, natural rabbit colonies, but man made hummocks and depressions intended to provide a source of fresh meat when needed. They offered natural cover, and it was probably this outcrop of scrub in otherwise arable terrain that the pioneers had to clear to facilitate movement of the cavalry. Captain Stewart noted that early in the day of July 2nd, the Royalists had endeavoured to seize this Bream/warren area and had been forced off. It was Stewart's contention that the Royalists saw in this area a position which gave them 'Sun and winde of us', which means that as the sun moved into the west, it would have shone from behind forces established on the Bream. Thus successful Royalist occupation of that point would have turned the allied flank before battle was joined, might thereby induce a premature engagement, and result in allied defeat. Once the Bream was firmly under allied control, pioneers were employed to clear it for better deployment of the allied horse on that wing.

Stewart, writing of the Royalist position fronting the allied left on Bilton Bream, stated that they were drawn up behind a 'cross ditch' which was manned with musketeers. Firth, quoting a secondary source, referred to the deployment of the Royalist right wing behind 'a warren and a slough'. Clearly, the warren and that occupied by Cromwell near Bilton Bream are one and the same, and this terrain feature lay between the two armies at the Tockwith end of the battlefield. Slough, however, ordinarily taken as meaning a bog or a stretch of marshy land, has an alternative 17th century meaning as a ditch or a drain. Thus it is likely that Firth's source alluding to a 'slough' and Stewart's allusion to a 'cross ditch' refer to one terrain feature. This ditch, still in existence, but probably deeper and wider before enclosure, served as the parish boundary between Tockwith and Long Marston at this point of the moorland.

On the Royalist side, north of the Long Marston/Tockwith road and close to the village of Tockwith, the ditch, hitherto running directly south, curves sharply to the south-west and so runs for approximately 200 yards at an angle to Bilton Bream. This would appear as a cross ditch to forces on the Bream, and would have to be cleared by any advance down from the Bream. What precisely occurred here will be discussed in Chapter 4.

There is an apocryphal story concerning the battle which is best dealt with in the course of general remarks on terrain. Prince Rupert, it was alleged, being worsted in the battle on the Royalist right wing (as he was) took refuge in a bean field where, it is supposed, he concealed himself amongst bean plants face down in the mud until darkness gave him cover to escape. Alex Leadman identified the 'bean field' as lying on the west of Wilstrop Wood, which would be logical if the story must be treated with any credence. However, the source for the story (a prime example of London propaganda) alluded only to 'bean lands', which is not the same thing at all as a bean field. The point has a wider significance, in that the existence of a field anywhere on Marston Moor suggests cultivation for which, beyond the certainty of land under crops immediately to the north of the Long Marston/Tockwith road, cannot be supported from evidence. The term 'land' in the parlance of open field agriculture alludes to a strip of unenclosed arable or pasture in a complexity of such strips which would go to make up an open field. Such a 'land' would be found, in the context of Marston Moor, only in the town fields of Long Marston, Tockwith or Hessay. All of these are far removed from the vicinity of the defeat of Rupert's cavalry of the Royalist right wing: it may be that in the propaganda story is some subtle allusion now lost upon later readership. The essence of the point is that the moorland was simply that: open, common land with some enclosures on its periphery but these enclosures are manifestly not 'lands' in the contemporary sense.

The allied armies drew up their battle array with the advantage, to quote Lumsden, of 'ane sleeke and the hills', their troops standing or sitting in fields of corn, under a July sun, as the day grew heavy and threatened thunder and rain. From their vantage point they looked down upon their enemy 'a little below us' (Fairfax) on the moor 'commonly called Hesham Moore' (W. H.), mustering and deploying amidst 'ditches and sloughs of water' (Cholmeley). On the allied right Sir Thomas Fairfax would exercise his mind over the negotiation of the treacherous terrain with which he was confronted should it be the allies that would charge when battle began. He resolved the matter to some extent by deciding that he would commit his raw, inexperienced troops to the hazard, to take the first and most awful shock of natural obstacle and enemy musket fire. In the centre the allied infantry gradually perceived that their numerical advantage remained significant: so it would have seemed to Leven up at the Clump, hesitant and cautious but a soldier trained to exploit a weakness. On the allied left, Cromwell and the Eastern Association cavalry, rife with nascent Independency, determined Leven should not avoid battle on this occasion. Battle must have seemed a long time coming, but after an eventful day, at about 5 pm, it came.

PRELIMINARY MANOEUVRES

Prince Rupert was eager to give battle on July 1st and the Earl of Leven

55

was just as eager on that day to avoid it. However, Royalist manoeuvres on July 2nd suggest that Rupert, if he had not actually undergone a change of mind (which, in view of his moving his army across the Ouse, is extremely improbable) had at least bowed to pressure to postpone battle. But what were the Allied intentions on that day?

Breaking up their siege of York on June 30th, the Allies had withdrawn to the Marston Moor area expecting to have to fight Rupert should he approach by way of Boroughbridge. In purely numerical terms the Allied advantage was eroded by Rupert's advance on the city on the opposite side of the River Ouse and his effecting of a junction (at least, as the Allies believed) with the York garrison forces. After waiting for a day, July 1st, on the moorland, in debate as to what to do, the Allied high command was swayed by the Earl of Leven into abandoning their ground and marching off towards Tadcaster. Regardless of how this move might be argued in purely propaganda terms – whether in expectation of having to fight Rupert further south or drawing off to control the Ouse towards Selby – it was, in fact, a retreat. Simeon Ashe, chaplain to the Earl of Manchester, wrote that on the morning of July 2nd (and this must mean at around dawn) a party of Royalist cavalry appeared on the moor from the direction of York and, 'having faced us awhile, wheeled back out of sight'. It was at this juncture that Leven ordered the army to break camp, although probably in accordance with plans prepared overnight and not a spontaneous response to the sight of Rupert's cavalry. 'Hereupon our foot', continued Ashe, 'with Artillery, were commanded to advance towards Tadcaster. The Scots', comprising the van of the Allied army, 'being got almost to Tadcaster' and the infantry of the Eastern Association 'being two or three miles from Marston', they received suddenly a 'very hot alarum' that the Royalists, in strength, had returned to the moorland. At this point, the Earl of Leven ordered the entire army to retrace its steps to confront the Royalists. One of the problems attaching to this part of the day (all sources which mention it state that the cavalry of Rupert's advance guard appeared at about 9:00 am) is where, precisely, were the Allied generals? The speed of the Allied march is clear from Ashe, and others; Captain Stewart wrote that 'our Van was advanced within a mile of Tadcaster'; Douglas stated that 'some of our Scottish foot were advanced within half a mile of Todcastle'; Lumsden wrote 'our foot haffing the vanne we were not 1 myle from it'; Watson noted that the army was gone 'some five miles toward Cawood' and 'was with much difficultie to be brought backe'. Stockdale added the detail that the Allied carriages had also moved off in rear of the infantry. What is clear is that the bulk, if not all, of the Allied cavalry under Thomas Fairfax, Cromwell and Leslie remained on the moor as a rearguard to cover the retreat – 'the horse still kept the guards upon Hesseymore', wrote Stockdale. The latter, however, implied that Leven, Lord Fairfax and Manchester were also in the vicinity of the moor: 'the three Generalls all continued about Long Marston, where they had quartered all night'. The official Despatch of the senior generals, however, indicates plainly that by 9:00 am they had themselves abandoned the area, and were moving off with the carriages towards Tadcaster, leaving their lt.-generals in the rear. 'The armies being so far on their way', the Despatch stated, 'that the van was within a mile of' Tadcaster, 'notice was sent *us* by our horsemen [my emphasis] who were upon our rear', that the Royalist army was advancing. This was confirmed by Sir Thomas Fairfax who wrote that 'we [himself, Cromwell and Leslie] sent word to the Generals, of the necessity of making a stand'. The cavalry commanders had supposed, perhaps wrongly, that the appearance of the Royalist army on the moor meant that, unless the Allied army was brought back and put into order, they would be attacked in column of march and put in risk of destruction in a running fight. Leven had no option but to return.

The unidentified W.H., whose account is valuable for events early in the day particularly, was one of the Allied cavalrymen in the rearguard. He wrote: 'On Tuesday the second of July we pitcht in Hesham-Moore, where no sooner looking about us, but the enemy with displayed colours entered the same place bending towards the left hand by som reason of some advantage they perceived there; which we striving to prevent, made for it, before they should possess themselves of it; in the meantime [their] main body . . . pitcht in that very place and neare unto it which we left'. Sir Thomas Fairfax, having sent warning to Leven, remembered that 'by the advantage of the ground we were on' he 'hoped to make it good till they came back to us'. Cholmeley mentioned 'continual skirmishes between the horse which were in rear and van of the two armies'.

What took place at 9:00 am and immediately afterwards was a desultory struggle for advantages of terrain. Established on the moorland itself, the allied cavalry probably occupied a position between Moor Lane to their left and, to their right, the Hatterwith enclosures, which would give them a commanding view of the routes from York onto the moor. As soon as the Royalist colours appeared with a cavalry vanguard, as W.H. makes clear, the Allied cavalry drew back, moving towards the elevated ground of the ridge. It was also the intention of the Royalists to secure a footing on that same ridge. 'Bending towards the left hand', W.H. wrote, they endeavoured to gain 'some advantage they perceived there'. Captain Stewart was even more explicit: 'the Enemy perceiving that our Cavalry had possessed themselves of a corn hill, and having discovered neer unto that hill a place of great advantage, where they might have both Sun and Winde of us, advanced thither with a Regiment of Red Coats and a party of Horse'. It was Cromwell's cavalry which countered this move and secured the Bream: 'we sent out a party which beat them off, and planted there our left wing of Horse', Stewart added. Sir Henry Slingsby, who was still in York with the Marquess of Newcastle at this time, saw a body conveyed back to the city, that of Captain Roger Houghton,[5] and later learned the brief facts of the Bream fight: 'The enemy makes some shot at [the Prince's men] as they were drawing up into Battalio, & ye first shot kills a son of Sr Gilbert Houghton y^t was Captn in ye prince's army.' Captain Houghton was in fact a troop commander in the regiment of Richard Viscount Molyneux, a regiment which formed a part of the cavalry contingent brought north by Rupert and which was to be established on the Royalist right wing in the battle. Some writers have ascribed Houghton's death to the brief bombardment which took place in the mid-afternoon, but since he was removed from the field and buried in York during the course of July 2nd, that seems highly unlikely. His death during the struggle for control of the Bilton Bream was probably due to an exchange of pistol or carbine fire, Cromwell having some Scottish dragoons with him. That struggle was the first blood of the battle, and resulted in an Allied success.

While this action was taking place, and while the Allied cavalry made sure of their control of the ridge, the bulk of the Royalist army progressively filed onto the moorland to take up position. It was probably at this juncture, given the unexpected resistance, that Sir Bernard de Gomme, acting in the role of a modern staff officer, sketched out the intended deployment of the Royalist army, dictated to him by

Rupert, and evolved in the light of the failure to find more suitable ground. In view of the fact that the York infantry were not then to hand, de Gomme allowed for them to march up and to form a second and third line in the Royalist centre, but between 10:00 am and late afternoon the Royalist centre was spread very thinly indeed.

It has been implied that Rupert did not intend to force a battle until his infantry were intact. The fear that he might fall upon the Allied columns, which had prompted the 'hot alarum' for them to turn back, may have had no basis whatever beyond the natural interpretation of events by the cavalry lt.-generals. The Diary, a Royalist source, states that Rupert 'would have attaqued ye Enemy himself in their Retreat' but waited for the York infantry to come up to him. 'If ye P had falln upon ye Rear and miscarryd it would have been objected that he should have stayd for Newcastle.' Slingsby noted that Prince Rupert was under the impression that the Allies 'meant not to give battle'. If this is so, the attempt to take the Bream which was initially unoccupied would have been a move to force the Allied cavalry to abandon the ridge altogether and to fall back on their main column. The failure to take the Bream indicated firstly that the enemy was resolved to hold their ground and was, *ipso facto*, resolved to offer battle; and secondly, it obliged Rupert to adopt a more defensive stance than he may have originally intended. It is likely that at 9:00 am on the morning of July 2nd the Prince hoped to control the entire ridge and there to await the arrival of reinforcements, expected at any moment, before setting off in pursuit. In view of the delay of those reinforcements, of which the Allied commanders were certainly initially unaware, there was ample time for the enemy cavalry rearguard to cover the retreat. Unaware of this, and quite properly anticipating the danger of imminent attack, Thomas Fairfax, Cromwell and Leslie made efforts to secure the ridge and, by their unexpected action, forced Rupert to make the best of the moorland. Sir Hugh Cholmeley, putting forward possible reasons for the eventual Royalist defeat, wrote: 'The Prince's army, or ever he was aware was drawn too near the enemy, and into some place of disadvantage, which may be imputed rather to his commanders that had the leading of his van and marshalling of his forces than to himself.' The 'commanders that had the leading of his van', anticipating little if any resistance, in failing to take the Bream when confronted by the Eastern Association cavalry, let the initiative slip, as it turned out irretrievably, to the Allies;

and undermined at a single blow Royalist tactical ideas.

As the day wore on and the Allied forces returned to line the higher ground, the recovery of that initiative for Rupert would depend upon the speed with which the reinforcements from York would arrive, and a corresponding lack of alacrity on the Allied part. Hence, putting his men 'in such order as he intend'd to fight', Slingsby noted he was 'sending away to my Ld Newcastle to march wth all speed'. Slingsby was in York at this time, and his observation further supports the view that the Marquess himself had not left the city until gone 10:00 am. The Diary records that Rupert 'sent messages to ye Earle [sic] from time to time'. Rupert's agitation may be imagined. To secure the ground on which he was, he hoped but briefly, forced to deploy, he 'by divers regiments of Muskettiers so lined the hedge and ditch betwixt' his forces and the ridge that, to further quote Simeon Ashe, 'our Souldiers could not assault them, without very great apparent prejudice'. Whether full regiments performed this function, or, as is more likely, detachments from each regiment were sent forward to man the ditch, hedge or bank directly parallel to their positions, this unusual device was strictly defensive. It indicated to the Allied commanders, who from their vantage point could see clearly what was happening, that they need expect no frontal assault for the time being, and whether or not they were aware of the absence of a large body of Royalist foot, they must have perceived how thinly the foot were spread. Given time and a little luck the Allied army would be arrayed and their numerical superiority firmly re-established.

The Marquess of Newcastle arrived on the moor with his Lifeguard and probably with some infantry sometime between 10:00 am and 12 noon, probably nearer to the latter hour. As has been shown, he intended to have brought with him the York foot, but had been obliged to leave Lord Eythin to rally them in the city and to follow on. 'My Lord,' Rupert, according to Cholmeley, said to the Marquess, 'I wish you had come sooner with your forces, but I hope we shall yet have a glorious day.' Informed of the strong probability that the infantry would be further delayed, Rupert, according to Cholmeley, 'would with his own foot have been falling upon the enemy', intending to take advantage of the disorder on the ridge as the Allied foot came back from Tadcaster, but his proposal was apparently squashed by the Marquess and other officers. 'The Prince and my Lord', recorded the Duchess of

Newcastle, 'conferred with several of their officers, amongst whom there were several disputes concerning the advantages which the enemy had of sun, wind and ground.' The momentum of Rupert's march to York had been in serious danger of being lost during the acrimonious debates of July 1st. On the battlefield of Marston Moor, watching the enemy lining up and their numbers increasing steadily, further doubt, indecision and obstruction obliged the Prince to wait and hope that Eythin would bestir himself. If he had much faith in him it was thoroughly misplaced as, indeed, was Newcastle's.

Cholmeley recorded a criticism made of Prince Rupert in the wake of the defeat. 'Many do impute much to the Prince that he would engage to fight that day considering . . . many of the Marquesses foot were wanting.' Whoever was responsible for that piece of criticism did Rupert much less than justice. While it might be true that he should at least have allowed for a decision by the Allies to re-form in battle order, even given that eventuality there was no reason why victory could not still have gone to the Royalists if the York foot had left the city earlier than they did or, indeed, if Eythin had obeyed orders and had them mustered for march at 4:00 am. When these infantry did at length appear, at about 4:00 pm, Rupert was advised that it was too late to fight that day, and resolved to defer battle until the morning of the 3rd. After all, if Rupert had wanted to risk 14,000 men against 28,000 he could have done it on June 30th/July 1st with a far better psychological advantage than he possessed on July 2nd. Confident of his own abilities he may have been, but he was not a fool. He needed the York forces to offset numerical disadvantage. The dispiriting nature of the tedious wait for them to materialise may well have contributed to the decision to postpone battle. As it was, it was the Allies who 'engaged' to fight that day.

Between the fighting for the Bilton Bream, a struggle ineffectively prosecuted by Rupert's vanguard commanders, and approximately 2:00 pm when a cannonade was begun from the Allied lines, both armies were preoccupied in making good their ground and marshalling their forces. 'We were compelled to draw upon our Army, and to place it in battalio in a large field of Rie . . . being on a hill, we had the double advantage of the ground, and the wind', recorded Ashe, and wrote of Leven, Manchester and old Lord Fairfax riding about, marshalling their men as they marched back into line. In fact the Allied plan of battle reflected less a carefully evolved deployment of forces according to their relative strengths and experience, than simply the order in which regiments returned to the battlefield. The three commanding generals taking an active part in marshalling strongly suggests that speed was of the essence, for at any moment the Royalist might attack, and there was little time for a judicious redeployment of units. Ashe reckoned that the main part of the army was not fully into position before 'two or three a clock', a tense and lengthy time. Stockdale believed that 'by 2 a clock afternoon' the Allied forces 'were all putt into order for a feight', anticipating a Royalist onslaught. It then gradually dawned upon the Allied generals that the Royalists 'with their Horse drawn up in both wings' and such infantry as they had 'in many small bodies bespread' were not intending to force the issue as yet.

Lumsden was more informative about the Allied dispositions: 'no possibilitie to have our foot up in two hours', he wrote, and so 'we keepedt the advantage of ane sleeke and the hills with our horse till the foot as they came up were put in order'. At 'about two of the clock we had indifferently well formed our army', wrote Watson, 'and the great Ordnance of both sides began to play'. Waiting for the infantry, Lumsden stated that: 'In the mean tyme we advanced our canon and entred to play on them on the left wing, which maid them a littell to move; which they persaving brocht up thairs and gave us the lyk.'

ORDNANCE

Cannon balls recovered from the moor indicate that the most common gun on the Allied side was the Saker. This was a middling size gun suited for field work, with a prescribed calibre of 3½ inches, firing a ball of approximately 5 to 6 lbs. The point-blank range of such a gun was a mere 360 yards, but at a 10 degree elevation was capable of firing over 2,000 yards. The largest cannon present on the ridge, for which the evidence consists of a single 15 lb cannon ball found to the rear of the Royalist centre, was the Culverin, with a range of 2,650 yards at a 10 degree elevation. The primary damage done by a cannon ball, if it did not make its first impact on horse or man, and sometimes even if it did, resulted from the deflection of the missile after striking the ground, to which troops in close order were particularly susceptible. Cannon could also be used to fire case shot, ordinarily wooden boxes stuffed with scrap iron, nails, musket balls and other metallic rubbish and stones which, upon impact with the ground, burst, giving a shrapnel effect. One casualty amongst the Royalists was Thomas Danby, a Roman Catholic country gentleman from South Cave in the East Riding of Yorkshire, and in his late 40's. His fate was recorded by Mrs. Thornton: 'that poore gentleman was shot to death with a cannon bullet, and cutt off by the midst of his body, he being locked in his sadle that very day'. Thomas Danby was riding as a gentleman volunteer in a northern regiment, and his eldest son was a major elsewhere on the moor. This fatality indicates that the cannonade was more general than the sources might seem to imply, for Danby must have been on the Royalist left wing, and cannon balls have indeed been found in that area of the Atterwith Lane. Further, if Danby was indeed tied into his saddle for better securing his seat, it looks as if the Royalist army as a whole was standing to its arms throughout the day, ready for any eventuality. It is impossible to comment upon the frequency of the practice of locking a man into his saddle, save that it was a matter of choice.

The precise duration of the bombardment is unclear. It certainly began at about 2:00 pm, and it may be that the 'showers of rain which then fell' (Ashe), perhaps an hour or so later, dampened the powder so causing the Allies, as Slingsby noted, 'after 4 shots made' to 'give over'. He called the cannonade 'only a shewing their teeth'. Yet the sources do not all agree that the bombardment had so little effect. Douglas wrote that 'In the afternoon our cannon played upon their right wing, their cannon played back againe: God preserved me, their cannon coming very near me.' (Douglas, evidently, rode under David Leslie in the rear of the Allied left wing.) Stockdale alluded to a localised bombardment, stating 'part of them drawn up within shot of our Ordinance, which about 2 a'clock begann to play upon the Brigade of Horse that were nearest, and did some execution upon them'. Yet, the artillery duel proving to have had 'small success to either' (Watson), at about 'five of the clock wee had a generall silence on both sides'. This ominous stillness must have followed an episode recorded by Sir Henry Slingsby, who had come to the moor with Newcastle's Lifeguard. He wrote that when the guns fell silent, the enemy forces 'fell to singing Psalms' in Marston Fields. Nothing is more evocative of that tense, warm, damp July day than the voices of the Allied army rolling out across the flat moorland, over the heads of the Royalists there assembled, borne on the wind which blew in the Allies' favour. Straggling units were still

63

coming in, finding their place in the Allied lines.

THE FINAL MOVES

Ogden stated flatly that Eythin and the York foot did not appear until '4 of yᵉ Clocke in the afternoone', with which Cholmeley agreed. 'In the afternoon General King (i.e. Eythin) brings up the Marquess's foot, of which yet many were wanting, for here was not above 3,000'. Eythin, riding ahead of his forces as their general, joined the Prince and probably the Marquess in rear of the Royalist army, at or near Four Lanes Meet, which firm lanes offered means of rapid communication with each part of the Royalist array. 'The Prince demanded of King how he liked the marshalling of the army, who replied he did not approve of it being drawn too near the enemy, and in a place of disadvantage.' Whether or not Cholmeley was paraphrasing Eythin's comments and generally toning them down we do not know, but any such observation from Eythin, whose active role in the failures of the earlier part of the day was more than apparent to everyone, cannot but have aroused further ill feeling. 'Then said the Prince', Cholmeley went on, 'they may be drawn to a further distance'. Eythin stated that no, that was not feasible, it was too late.

There then followed a renewed discussion as to whether to begin the battle immediately, as the York infantry progressively filed into position. Cholmeley was adamant: 'It is so, King dissuaded the Prince from fighting . . . it was so near night.' The Duchess of Newcastle, who in all her account of the battle studiously avoided mentioning her husband's chief adviser, wrote that the Marquess 'asked his Highness what service he would be pleased to command him; who returned this answer, that he would begin no action upon the enemy till early in the morning' of the 3rd. There is nothing in what is known of this conference to support the contention that Newcastle was deprived of any field command whatsoever, or that he was slighted by Prince Rupert as a result of the latter's resentment at the way in which his orders had been seriously disobeyed. The Prince, who had lost the initiative, merely postponed consideration of what to do until later. No source suggests, and there is no way of knowing, how Rupert would have approached battle on July 3rd, but it is evident that very serious consideration was given to the predicament of the Royalist army. Is it

THE EARL OF NEWPORT WITH BARON GORING,
*c.*1635–40,

PRINCE RUPERT OF BAVARIA,
*c.*1641

possible that, given the fact of postponement of battle for a further 12 hours or more, the Royalists might have endeavoured to withdraw? Or to try to outflank the ridge? Or simply launch a frontal assault? Whatever, the distribution of commands could be left until tactics were decided upon. Advising Newcastle to 'repose himself', which he did by going 'to rest in his coach' which stood at hand on the moor, Rupert gave further order 'to have provisions for his army brought from York'. Eythin believed and Rupert also agreed that the enemy would make no attempt upon them in view of the lateness of the hour 'so that when the alarum was given, he was set upon the earth at meat a pretty distance from his troops and many of the horsemen were dismounted and laid on the ground' (Cholmeley). 'Not long had my Lord been in his coach', wrote the Duchess, 'but he heard a great noise and thunder of shooting, which have him notice of the armies being engaged'.

Given Eythin's arrival on the field at about 4:00 pm, riding ahead of his York infantry, the bulk of the latter cannot either have been on the moor, let alone disposed according to de Gomme's plan, until after 5:00 pm at the earliest. It is highly probable that some regiments, and one in particular, the Northern foot of Colonel Sir William Lambton (see Chapter 5) were standing in rank and file to the rear of the Royalist left wing, having debouched onto the moor from the track that ran from Micklegate Bar via Hessay. The Earl of Leven, obliged to return by the pressure put upon his rearguard earlier in the day, watching events with his commanders, observed two singular occurrences: the arrival of reinforcements belatedly from York, and not yet deployed fully, and secondly the relaxation of alertness as sections of the Royalist army were advised that battle was deferred and that rations would be distributed. Riders were sent towards York to bring out the supply train. These events offered Leven an opportunity to exploit his advantages of position. The Allied sources which mention the time of advance from the ridge, Watson, Ashe, Grifen, W.H., and the official Despatch, vary in ascribing this event to between 5:00 pm and 8:00 pm. Since time would be estimated from the position of the sun, and since we know that it was a wet and cloudy day, an attempt to pinpoint a precise time for the commencement of the battle from the sources themselves would be fruitless. What is beyond doubt is that, between 5:00 pm and 7:00 pm, the Royalist position took on a new aspect, and the Earl of Leven sent his army forward to capitalise upon it.

'We advanced about 200 paces towards the Enemy, our Canon (which had plaid one or two houres before from the top of the Hill) was drawne forward for our best advantage', wrote Ashe. 'The signe being given we marched down to the charge. . . . Wee came down the hill in the bravest order, and with the greatest resolution' (Watson). 'It was resolved we should advance down the hill throch ane great feild of corne to ane ditch, which they had in possession, which it pleased God to prosper that they wer put from it' (Lumsden).

'The reason why they fell thus suddenly upon the Prince, as many conjecture', Cholmeley wrote, 'is that a Scottish officer amongst the Prince his horse, whilst the armies faced one another, fled to the Parliament army and gave them intelligence; and it was further observed that Hurry a Scotchman having the marshalling of the horse on the Prince's right wing, his own troop were the first that turned their backs; yet I have heard the Prince in his own private opinion did not think Hurry culpable of infidelity.' It is a curious feature of the history of the military side of the civil war that defeat was often ascribed to treachery by some individual. Hurry's unfortunate career as a turncoat,[6] although he died as a Royalist, executed for his part with Montrose in Scotland, made him a natural scapegoat. There is also some similarity, superficially, between Cholmeley's statement and that contained in the Somerville account treated in the Introduction. If it were true that Hurry's was the first troop to flee the field (see Chapter Four) that in itself were no evidence of treachery, and stories such as this should always be treated with the gravest suspicion as indicating less a reality than a frame of mind amongst the defeated.

There was anyway little 'intelligence' that a traitor could convey to the enemy. By virtue of their position on the ridge everything that transpired beneath them would be apparent, including the relaxation of alertness when rations were fetched. As will anyway be seen, Sir John Hurry himself, whatever his soldiers did, remained on the moor and was there at the very end of the battle, or nearly so, when he met a Royalist eye-witness and cavalry commander, Sir Philip Monckton.

'Our army in its severall parts moving downe the Hill, was like unto so many thick clouds . . . the enemy was amazed and daunted.' Thus Ashe remembered the scene which he doubtless observed from the area of the Clump. That the Royalists may have indeed been 'amazed and daunted' can be imagined, but that they stood to their arms, for the

66

most part, will be seen. Some 46,000 men closed with each other, sword and lance, pike and musket, with several reputations in the balance and much political capital at stake. Of these, some 4,000 and more would lie dead upon the field by morning, and hundreds, probably thousands, would die of wounds in ensuing days and weeks. Many would be crippled for life. Quarter Sessions and Petty Sessions all over England and Wales would be petitioned for a generation by men seeking financial relief who had been blinded or lost arms or legs on Marston Moor. Oliver Cromwell's reputation and standing as a soldier and a politician would be based upon a prodigious slaughter of the ungodly.

NOTES

1. For Wilstrop village, see Beresford, M., *The Lost Villages of England*, 1963 reprint, pp. 301/306 and *passim*.
2. This track survives in part at the eastern end of Hessay village. It was destroyed piecemeal during enclosures of the 18th century, but in Hessay a boundary marker limiting the extent of the powers of the parish constables of Poppleton survives to mark its route. See Newman, P., 'Absentee Landlords and the Enclosure of the Open Fields: Hessay in the Ainsty', *York Historian*, 3, 1980.
3. The Hatterwith enclosures, the existence of which is evidenced by papers of 1633 from the Long Marston parish chest (deposited in the Borthwick Institute of Historical Research, York), had been taken in from the moor by the Thwaites family, Lords of Marston, *c.* 1560 and had been a matter of dispute. The hedgerows marking their position have been partially destroyed. They were the only verifiable enclosures on the moor in 1644, and their proximity to the route from Hessay is important. 'White Syke Close' was created after 1766 in the process of enclosure on Marston Moor, and almost certainly did not exist in 1644. The idea that White Syke Close played an important part in the battle is an invention of the 19th century, when battle studies were superficial in their treatment of sources.
4. A. H. Woolrych made a serious effort to locate the 1766 Enclosure Map for Long Marston, which remains unlocated since he hoped to be able to explain what befell Sir Thomas Fairfax on the Allied right wing: 'One of the obscurer points of the battle'. See correspondence of 1959 in the York City Archives.
5. Captain Houghton was Colonel Sir Gilbert Houghton's third son, and came from Houghton Tower in Lancashire. For his burial in York Minster on July 2nd, see Skaife, R. H., ed: *The Register of Burials in York Minster*, York 1870.
6. For Hurry, see Dictionary of National Biography. Major General Hurry or Urry changed sides three times during the civil wars, but he was a professional soldier whose experience would outweigh any dislike of his moral duplicity.

Chapter 4

BATTLE 1:
'AS STUBBLE TO OUR SWORDS'

'Truly England and the Church of God hath had a great favour from the Lord, in this great Victory given unto us, such as the like never was since this War began. . . . We never charged but we routed the enemy.'[1] In this way, on Friday July 5th, Oliver Cromwell sent word of the battle of Marston Moor to a kinsman, Colonel Valentine Walton. It was a very personal view, in that the experiences of the Allied commanders on the whole were by no means as happy as his. The obelisk, erected on the battlefield in 1936 by the Cromwell Association, accorded the battle honours almost exclusively to their idol. Forty years after, a second plaque, intended to redress the balance, bestowed praise on Sir Thomas Fairfax, but on very unsound historical grounds. Many field and regimental commanders on both sides fought better at Marston Moor than Fairfax did. It is certain that Cromwell need share the honours of Allied victory with no one.

Two giants of the civil war years confronted each other on July 2nd, Cromwell himself and the more flamboyant Prince Rupert. It was a dramatic confrontation but its importance is often misinterpreted. On the eve of battle Oliver Cromwell was a fairly well-known Member of Parliament, holding the rank of Lt.-General of the Horse in the army of the Eastern Association by dint of his leadership qualities. Rupert knew of him, but had no great reason to either fear or revere him as an enemy. Until Marston Moor, Cromwell's military record was no better, and no worse, than that of many a country-gentleman turned soldier in either army. At Marston Moor, he made his name, and established himself as Prince Rupert's superior in the tactics of the battlefield. The two generals looked upon each other's colours and recognised each other's presence; for Rupert, however, the person of Cromwell assumed ominous qualities as a consequence of the battle. On the personal level,

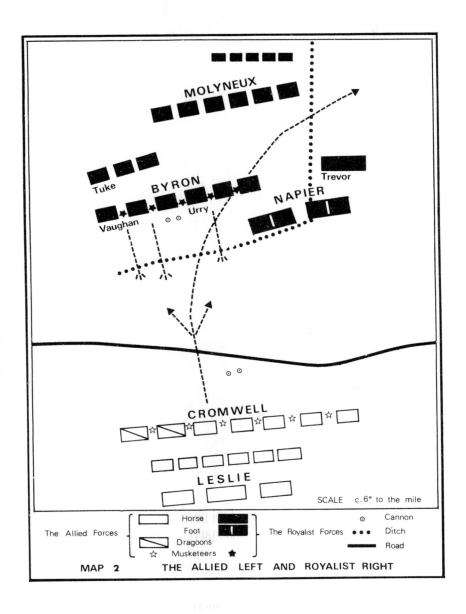

MOLYNEUX

Tuke

BYRON

Trevor

Vaughan

Urry

NAPIER

CROMWELL

LESLIE

SCALE c. 6" to the mile

The Allied Forces

Horse

Foot

Dragoons

☆ Musketeers ★

The Royalist Forces

⊙ Cannon

●●● Ditch

━━ Road

MAP 2   THE ALLIED LEFT AND ROYALIST RIGHT

Marston Moor saw the rise of one general and the beginning of the eclipse of another.

To ascribe Cromwell's personal triumph solely to sound tactical thinking would, however, be unwise. Preconceived notions of tactics must allow for the degree of the unknown when it comes to implementing them. No small part of Cromwell's success lay in the mistakes of his immediate opponents on the Royalist right wing, and in Rupert's inability to restore order to that wing. It would also be true to say that when a section of Rupert's cavalry did bring Cromwell's cavalry to a halt, they assisted him quite unintentionally in his tactical plans. But Cromwell was victorious because he kept his cavalry together, making them operate under tight control.

The dispositions of the forces of the Allied left and Royalist right wings will be clear from Map 2. Rupert in fact employed an unconventional deployment of his cavalry. The cross ditch lying between the Royalist right wing and the Allies on the rising ground to their south, was partially manned by musketeers under Colonel Thomas Napier,[2] and to their rear and left was the cavalry regiment of Colonel Marcus Trevor.[3] Napier's musketeers and pikemen, positioned in such a way, gave support to the cavalry of the Royalist right, and utilised the ditch as a means of cover for themselves in an otherwise exposed, forward position. To Napier's rear and right were the bodies of the Royalist front line commanded by John Lord Byron[4] and comprising the regiments of, from Napier's right moving west, Sir William Vaughan,[5] Sir John Urry (to whom we shall return) and Byron himself. On the right flank of Byron's forces, that is, to their rear and right, was the Duke of York's regiment under its colonel, the Essex-born and future playwright, Samuel Tuke. His task was to cover the exposed flank of the front line, and to assault the flank of any enemy advance. Further to the rear Richard Viscount Molyneux commanded the reserve, composed of his own regiment, and those of Colonels Thomas Tyldesley and Thomas Leveson.[6] Probably to the rear of Molyneux, lay the regiment of Horse of Prince Rupert himself. Byron's front line was further strengthened by detachments of commanded musketeers interspersed between his bodies of horse.

On the Bilton Bream and the coney warren and east of it were the cavalry of the Allied front line under Cromwell which, like Byron's, were interspersed with bodies of musketeers. This employment of infantry as support for horse was duplicated across the moor on the Allied right and Royalist left, a development intended to impede an enemy cavalry charge and to deprive it of momentum by musket fire. It was conventional tactics, but Rupert's positioning of Napier's infantry in the cross-ditch, and his use of musketeers to line the obstacle between arable and moor land, was improvisation. He hoped both to utilise natural obstacles in the terrain, and to cover his army where it was weakest either numerically, or in its deployment. Brigadier Young, however, has stressed that it is unwise to be dogmatic about tactical decisions taken so long ago. The deployment ordered by Rupert looks to have been essentially defensive, although musketeers amongst cavalry had both a defensive and an offensive role depending upon circumstances.

The extreme left of Cromwell's front line was composed of Colonel Hugh Fraser's Scottish dragoons, mounted infantry armed with carbines. Regarded somewhat slightingly by real cavalry, the dragoons rode to the place of action, but that mobility was intended to facilitate their rapid deployment to fight on foot. They might be considered as a form of commando unit. Their task would be to flush out pockets of Royalist infantry hampering deployment of the cavalry proper, and they were no doubt thus positioned in order to deal with Napier's musketeers in the ditch. The regiments which made up Cromwell's first and second lines, all Eastern Association cavalry, cannot be identified for sure. The third and rearmost line, a reserve, consisted of the cavalry regiments of David Leslie, commander of that reserve, Kircudbright in the centre, and Balcarres on the right.[7] It has been pointed out that the Eastern Association accounted for the bulk of the Allied cavalry, and so, with Leslie's Scots, the Allied left consisted of in excess of 5,000 mounted men, plus units of infantry. The Royalist right wing facing them numbered perhaps 3,000 or so plus 500 infantry. 'Upon the left Wing of Horse was the Earl of Manchester's whole cavalry', wrote Stewart, 'and three regiments of the Scottish horse.' The wisdom of Rupert's covering dispositions in face of this numerically superior force is evident.

A further attempt by the Prince to bolster his right wing was recorded by Edmund Ludlow. Ludlow, a Republican opponent of Cromwell, and not himself present at Marston Moor, was nevertheless objective in his treatment of the battle and of Cromwell's role in it. He stated that 'the enemy commanded by Prince Rupert, had gained an advantageous piece of ground upon Marston Moor, and caused a battery to be erected upon it. . . . Whereupon Col. Cromwell commanded two field-pieces to be brought in order to annoy the enemy, appointing two regiments of foot to guard them; who marching to that purpose, were attacked by the foot of the enemy's right wing, that fired thick upon them from the ditches.' Behind Napier's position in the cross-ditch the ground rises to a hummock, and then drops again onto the level moorland beyond, where Byron's cavalry were disposed. That hummock provided sufficient elevation for the small battery to be positioned upon it, and the guns were probably moved up during the afternoon, perhaps during the bombardment. To obviate the need to charge into the battery, Cromwell ordered up guns with which to try to knock it out, and in the process his gunners and their escort (surely not two entire regiments?) came under fire from Napier's men. As events were to turn out, Byron was effectively to block the fire of his own battery anyway, but Cromwell's move was tactically right even though it probably gave warning to Byron of intended general action. Moreover, the bringing up of the two field guns had demonstrated the danger posed by the Royalist musketeers in the cross-ditch; when battle was joined, Fraser's dragoons were sent to deal with that ditch immediately. These 'acted their part so well, that at the first assault they beate the enemy from the ditch, and shortly after killed a great many' (Stewart).

The numerical weakness of the Royalist right wing is obvious. It is also clear that Prince Rupert was only too well aware of that, and that his infantry deployment and positioning of the battery were attempts to remedy it. Much of the evidence for what befell the Royalist right when battle was joined comes from sources hostile to them. Royalist accounts tend to be confusing, or to gloss over a disaster. As overall commander, Rupert could not himself spend the day sitting on the right wing, and he was probably with his Lifeguard troop in the area of the lane running west from Four Lanes Meet. According to the *Life of James II*[8] first published 1816, 'the day had in all probablity been the king's, if the Lord Byron had punctually obeyed his orders'. Byron commanded the Royalist right in Rupert's absence, and although his impetuosity and unreliability were well known, his seniority required that Rupert should defer to it. The improvisations ordered by the Prince to strengthen Byron's position were carried a stage further by explicit orders for Byron to obey. It was an attempt to curtail the latter's propensity for acting first and thinking afterwards. 'Prince Rupert had posted him very advantageously behind a warren and a slough, with a positive command not to quit his ground, but in that posture only to expect and receive there the charge of the enemy.' These orders were clearly contrary to every known precept of cavalry action, for cavalry which meets a charge at the standstill is doomed to be broken by the sheer weight of the enemy, let alone by numerical superiority. In giving such an order, Rupert intended not simply to restrain Byron from doing anything premature, but also to take full advantage of the lie of the land. The *Life* goes on: 'the enemy . . . must necessarily be much disordered in passing over to him, as being to receive the fire of 700 musketiers in their advance to him, which undoubtedly had been very dangerous, if not ruinous, to them'. In other words, if Byron had 'punctually obeyed' his orders, then in an advance by Cromwell and the Eastern Association cavalry, the latter would have had to face concentrated musketry fire from the cross-ditch and from musketeers amongst the Royalist horse, as well as cannon fire from the battery on the hummock. Under this pressure, with such support as they could get from their dragoons and musketeers, the Eastern Association cavalry would have had to force a crossing of the ditch, regroup beyond it, and then charge. Byron's orders, followed to the letter, would have involved the Allied left wing in a potential disaster equivalent to that which actually befell the Allied right (see Chapter 5). Given their numerical superiority, it might well have been possible for Cromwell to force the ditch and to regroup, but they would have been seriously depleted in numbers and perhaps in morale, and have then come under attack from Byron's waiting horse. That is what ought to have happened, and if it had, then, as the *Life* stated, the day would 'in all probability' have belonged to Prince Rupert.

'Instead of maintaining his post', the *Life* goes on, 'as he ought in duty to have done, when the enemy had only drawn down two or three field pieces, and with them played upon him, he suffered himself to be persuaded by Colonel Hurry to march over the morass and charge them, by which inconsiderate action he gave them the same advantage which he had formerly over them; for they charging him in his passage over the ground already mentioned, he was immediately routed'. This view was supported by Thomas Fuller, though by no means a primary source, in his *Worthies*.[9] Fuller, a Royalist chaplain who knew something about fighting, wrote of Byron that 'A right valiant Lord severed (and in some

73

sort secured) with a ditch from the enemy, did not attend till foe forced their way unto him, but gave his men the trouble to pass over the ditch; the occasion of much disorder' – not least, to the musketeers in that ditch, obliged to make way. The Diary states 'Lord Byron then made a Charge upon Cromwell's forces' and notes 'Reprsent here ye Posture the P. put ye forces in and how ye improper charge of ye Lord Byron much harm was done'.

Failure and defeat generally encourage a search for scapegoats and Fuller reiterated the charge against Urry that he influenced Byron to disobey orders, even going so far as to write of 'foul play herein'. In this view of events, Urry 'divided the King's old horse, so valiant and victorious in former fights, in small bodies alleging this was the best way to break the Scottish lancers. But those horse, always used to charge togther in whole regiments or greater bodies, were much discomposed with this new mode so that they could not find themselves'. All that happened, probably, is that the Royalists broke order and formation in order to cross the ditch. It is improbable that Byron, from what is known of his character, needed any urging to move. Believing soundly in his own erring judgement, he turned every advantage which he had, so meticulously prepared for him by Rupert, against himself. Lord Byron gave Oliver Cromwell the battle on a plate.

In brief, this is what happened. The Earl of Leven, seeing the belated arrival of the York infantry on the moor (a point stressed very strongly by Arthur Trevor) resolved to attack. He chose a time of reorganisation in the Royalist centre, a time when psychologically the Royalists were preparing to spend a night on the moor. Orders to this effect were sent to commanders on either wing of the Allied army, and in its centre. Cromwell, alert to dangers in Rupert's deployment, resolved to try to destroy the artillery opposed to him as quickly as he could, hoping also, no doubt, to keep down the heads of Napier's musketeers. Two or three field guns were hurried forward by their gunners and teams, helped by covering fire from musketeers sent with them. The Royalist musketeers in the cross ditch opened fire on the teams, probably with some success. This sudden movement would have been interpreted by Byron as the start of the battle (which in a sense it was), and may have given rise to the idea that Cromwell on his own initiative began the action. As rapidly as possible, the Allied field guns were positioned and perhaps a few volleys shot off. The

Royalist cavalry, coming under bombardment for the second time that day, and convinced that battle was begun, looked to Byron. After several hours inactivity and enforced idleness, he was called upon to make a rapid decision which his orders did not require him to make. Swayed by the cavalry's restiveness, by concern for its morale, or by his own faith in himself, Byron threw his orders aside. He sent his front line of cavalry forward, probably with Tuke's regiment on their flank, and the musketeers amongst the cavalry moved forward as well. The artillery on the hummock was blocked. In the cross ditch, Napier's men rapidly moved apart and lost cohesion to permit their cavalry to cross, reform, and charge. That was the critical moment. To his relief and astonishment, Cromwell saw the hazards facing him virtually melt away. He counter-attacked. All the hazards threatening Cromwell's cavalry had been cut down to one: hand to hand fighting with the enemy cavalry already in some disorder. Most importantly, Napier's musketeers had been effectively silenced.

FIREARMS

The most common musket on both sides was the matchlock, fired from a rest rammed into the ground in front of the musketeer. Fusils or carbines, carried chiefly by dragoons or by the escorts of artillery columns, possessed a wheel-lock mechanism utilising a flint and steel as opposed to the smouldering match or taper of the matchlock, and were called 'firelocks'. Coming slowly into general use, but probably not common on Marston Moor, were flintlocks, known as 'snaphaunces' or English locks (see illustrations). Rate of loading and firing, and the effective concentration of fire, was more important than accuracy. The musket's range was reckoned at the time as between 416 yards and 200 yards,[10] the latter the furthest range at which musket fire could be deadly. Between 1834 and 1841 tests were carried out by the British government on smooth bore flintlocks of 0.752", comparable with the weapons available during the civil war, although it should be pointed out that the powder of the 19th century was purer than that of the 17th, and consequently a lesser quantity was used. It was found that at 150 yards a target twice the size of a man might be hit three times in every four shots, but beyond that range a score of nil was recorded. A target four times the size of a man, say, the size of a mounted cavalryman, set

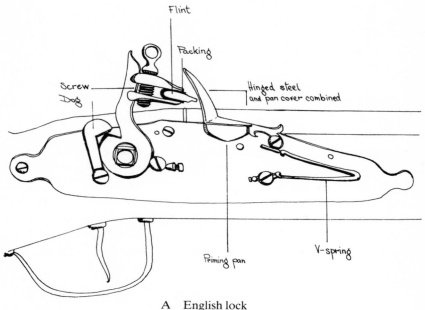

Flint

Packing

Screw

Dog

Hinged steel
and pan cover combined

V-spring

Priming pan

A   English lock

up at 250 yards could not be hit once in 10 shots, even though every precaution was taken to steady the weapon on a rest. So, giving Napier 500 muskets, the soldiers all veterans and able to reload and give fire rapidly either in unison or at random (perhaps every 45 seconds), then Cromwell's cavalry would have had to endure a vigorously concentrated fire becoming the more galling as the distance between the two sides shortened to less than 150 yards. Speed of reloading was crucial. Each musketeer wore over his shoulder and across his breast a bandolier from which hung, at his hip, a side arm. From this bandolier also hung twelve wooden or lead tubes, 'twelve apostles', each containing the measured charge to be poured into the musket barrel before insertion of the lead ball. The musketeer would thus have to empty the tube into the barrel, roll in a ball (often spat in from the mouth where two or three were kept ready), and then ram in with a rod a screw of paper or of cloth to hold the ball in place when the musket was levelled. From a container on his hip, which hung alongside a pouch of lead shot, the musketeer would then pour priming powder onto a pan beside the touch hole of the weapon. This would be ignited when the trigger was pulled and the serpentine holding the smouldering match, or the hammer gripping a

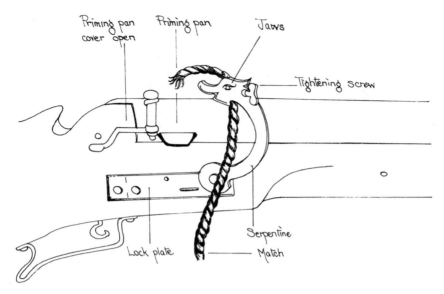

Priming pan cover open   Priming pan   Jaws   Tightening screw   Serpentine   Lock plate   Match

B   Matchlock

flint, was released. This was much the same method as that employed in loading and firing a pistol. Speed is relative, but Napier's men had been in sufficient campaigns to have mastered the art of rapid firing and reloading, and Cromwell's cavalry would have been soundly peppered with shot. As it was, Napier's men were now rendered useless to assist their cavalry. Several hundred muskets were, to all intents and purposes, silenced.

A musket was essentially a short-range weapon, but there can be no doubting its deadliness when the target was hit – cavalry breast-plates were not proof against musket shot. A soldier wounded by a sword stroke would, unless a main artery was severed or loss of blood too excessive, expect to recover. Musket balls, however, penetrating first dirty clothing and then flesh, would as often as not induce sepsis, and drive fragments of splintered bone into the wound. Moreover, a ball striking bone matter would be distorted and perhaps fracture in parts, so that if a man were not killed outright by a musket shot, there was every prospect of a lingering death from the wound sustained. Hundreds probably died after Marston Moor who were not buried on the field and consequently do not figure in the total of casualties.[11] Byron's precipitate charge effectively reduced Cromwell's casualty rate.

Gustavus Adolphus of Sweden, innovator on the battlefields of Europe, had broken away from the traditional method of cavalry charge. Now, instead of cavalry charging, halting, discharging their pistols, and then falling on with drawn swords, cavalry commanders relied upon the sheer impact of a headlong charge. The pistol, with a maximum range of from 120 to 150 yards, would be reserved for close melee fighting or for pursuit. It was not conventional tactics for cavalry to be deployed in a stationary defensive posture as Byron was ordered by Rupert. In disobeying orders, Byron acted conventionally but, in view of the disorder in which he put his men, and in view of his good defensive position and enemy superiority, he brought about his own ruin.

'Cromwell having ye left wing drawn into 5 bodies of horse, came off the Cony Warren, by Bilton Bream, to charge our horse, & upon their first charge rout'd y^m; they fly along by Wilstrop woodside as fast and as thick as could be' (Slingsby). Byron's horse broke, which was only to have been expected in the circumstances in which they were attacked, but while Cromwell was having a wound tended (an incident to be discussed later), Lord Molyneux and the Royalist second line stood their ground. Stockdale noted that Cromwell 'first' routed 'one regiment or body of horse of the enemyes'. Watson wrote 'the left wing of our Horse, led by Cromwell, which was to charge their right wing . . . in which was all their gallant men. . . . Our front divisions of Horse charged their front, [Cromwell's] division . . . in which himselfe was in person charged the first division' of Byron's. 'Cromwell's owne division had a hard pull of it; for they were charged . . . both in Front and Flank'. This flank attack must have been Tuke's little regiment in action. 'They stood at the sword's point a pretty while, hacking one another; but at last he brake through them, scattering them before him.' Perhaps this final break-through coincided with events on the other wing of the battlefield (see Chapter 5) where positions were reversed. Watson went on 'At the same instant the rest of our horse of that Wing', meaning Leslie's reserve line and perhaps the second line of Eastern Association cavalry, 'had wholly broken all . . . horse on their right Wing, and were in the chase of them'. This looks as if Byron's unfortunate front line, shattered by Cromwell's front line, was left to be mopped up by David Leslie whilst the Eastern Association cavalry moved on across the ditch, reformed, and came to blows with Molyneux. W. H. reckoned the action took 'lesse than an hour', which in view of numerical superiority and the disintegration of Byron's front line, indicates the hardness of the fighting when Cromwell and Molyneux came to grips. It ought here to be stressed that some of the Royalist cavalry which had crossed the protective ditch in Byron's charge, fought their way through Leslie's ranks and found themselves in the area of the Bream, battle having passed on and they too spent to act. Hurry was one of these (see Chapter 5). What became of Byron is nowhere recorded.

Lord Saye acknowledged the Royalist courage, certainly as a means of enhancing Cromwell's achievement, but showing that the Royalist horse did not break in one fell swoop by the Allies. 'The Enemies Horse, being many of them, if not the greatest part, Gentlemen, stood very firm a long time coming to a close fight with the Sword, and standing like an Iron Wall, so that they were not easily broken.' Thus, having more or less disposed of Byron's unfortunate front line, the Allied cavalry cleared the ditch and reformed to tackle Molyneux. Fraser's dragoons now proceeded to deal with the dis-ordered musketeers in the ditch, and Napier's men, deprived of any support, lacking all cohesion, were driven out and scattered, many of them being killed or taken. Byron had offered these veterans as a sacrifice on the altar of his own misjudgement. Napier's men, whose role in the battle as conceived by Rupert would have been crucial, were destroyed having achieved nothing. The enemy were upon them before they could themselves reform, and using their muskets as clubs, their side-arms, or simply running, it must have been a case of every man for himself. These, and the musketeers in Byron's front line, were simply thrown away.

The 'Iron Wall' of Molyneux's cavalry clashed with the successful Allies whilst Cromwell retired to have a wound dressed. Trevor, Tuke, Vaughan, Urry and the rest were all spent. Molyneux and his brother, Lt.- Colonel Caryll Molyneux, were Lancashire Roman Catholics, and Caryll had earned for himself a reputation as a killer of his enemies during Prince Rupert's march through Lancashire: a 'blud-thirsty Papest'. They were both young men. The Viscount was 24, Caryll 22, but they had been fighting since 1642. Sir Thomas Tyldesley ('a noble generous-minded Gentleman' was one Parliamentarian's description of him) had earned his knighthood in July 1643 by sheer personal courage at Burton-on-Trent. He, too, was a Roman Catholic, as was Thomas Leveson, the stubborn sheriff of Staffordshire who alarmed his fellow Royalists as much as his enemies. It is hardly surprising that these commanders should have made a concerted effort to halt Cromwell's numerically superior cavalry, nor should it be surprising that for a time they succeeded. The Allies had to reform north of the cross ditch, and Cromwell was briefly absent. Molyneux, no doubt desperate, must have sent urgent riders to Prince Rupert to summon up support. To emphasise the resistance of these men is not to deny the collapse of a good part of the right wing. The Duchess of Newcastle recorded the 'dismal sight of the horse of his Majesty's right wing, which out of a panic fear had left the field, and run away with all speed they could'. She stated that her husband, hurrying to his horse on first hearing the roar of battle begun, 'made them stand once, yet they immediately betook themselves to their heels again, and killed even those of their own party that endeavoured to stop them'. This portrays very serious demoralisation indeed, and there is no reason to doubt that Newcastle, who probably did try to check the rout, for he was a man of marked personal courage, was sadly impressed by their cowardice. Rupert, when battle began, was nowhere near the wing he intended to command. Had he been, things might have been different. Cholmeley wrote that 'Upon the alarum the Prince mounted to horse and galloping up to the right wing met his own regiment turning their backs to the enemy which was a thing so strange and unusual he said "Swounds, do you run, follow me." ' Rupert's own regiment, more tractable in his presence than the motley assembly of riders the Marquess had tried to turn back, faced about, and 'he led them to a charge, but fruitlessly, the enemy before having broken the force of that wing, and without any great difficulty'. Rupert saw Molyneux's cavalry hemmed in and probably giving ground, and no doubt also huge bodies of enemy horse crossing the ditch and building up Cromwell's strength to its north. Rupert's single regiment, even with the Prince at their head, could neither save Molyneux nor ward off the massive concentrations of enemy cavalry moving forward. Cholmeley, like Newcastle (from whom he must have drawn much of this section of his narrative) was nevertheless impressed by the 'panic fear' which 'I know not by what fate' had suddenly gripped 'troops which formerly had been thought unconquerable'.

Molyneux's regiments could not sustain the fight without help, and

The Pourtraicture of his Excellency Sr: Thomas
Farfax Generall of all the English forces for
the Service of yᵉ two houses of Parliament.

Guilᵐ Faithorne sculp:

OLIVER CROMWELL,
*c.*1649

help they would demonstrably not get. Everyone was running, as far as Molyneux was concerned, everyone in the entire Royalist army except his men, was running. He knew nothing of the Royalist success on the other wing, and even if he had known of it, it would mean little. Smoke, confusion, disorder, all told against appreciation of the battle as a whole. Leslie's cavalry were pressing on the rear of the fleeing right wing, and Molyneux's men, if they would not be encircled and taken, also had to break. Whether their withdrawal was commanded, or induced by individual decision, is not clear. They had not at first been infected with that panic remarked upon by Newcastle and Cholmeley, otherwise they would never have stood their ground at all. The onset of panic is an army's worst enemy, an ingredient for certain defeat. What is remarkable about Marston Moor is that this panic did not communicate itself beyond those specific sections of the field where it was manifest. Neither the Royalist centre infantry nor the cavalry of their left wing were infected. Byron's second line was almost certainly not infected. Similarly, panic in the Allied centre infantry and Allied right did not spread. The isolation of panic underlines the relative isolation in which component parts of each army fought in their section of the field, and stresses the lack of co-ordination induced by movement, circumstances, smoke and gathering darkness.

The ingredients of Royalist panic may, to a degree, be pinned down. Earlier in the morning the cavalry had swept onto the moor anticipating a glorious end to their glorious march to York. Over-confident, they had been beaten from ground they needed and had then been obliged to stand to their guard all day. Momentum was lost. Were they to expect to give battle? If so, when? Day wore on, anticipated reinforcements failed to appear, Allied numbers visibly increased on the ridge. Allied cannon fired into cavalry ranks in the afternoon, killing and wounding. It had rained, making for discomfort. Disagreement between Rupert and the Marquess and their officers, which must have been rumoured on July 1st, flared up again when Eythin, at last appearing on the field, further displayed his dislike for Rupert's plans and mistrust of his military judgement. Orders were given that there would be no battle that day. Rations were to be consumed or to be distributed. A long uncomfortable night lay ahead. Suddenly, there was shooting, and Allied movement. Cannon were brought up and aimed once again into the Royalist cavalry under Byron. Goaded, Byron made a foolish decision, contrary to all orders, relieving tension, reasserting a faded dominance. Barely begun, his front line's charge was rolled up by a general Allied counter-attack the sheer weight of which would have been terrifying, and the inevitability of which would have been predicted. Byron's line, disordered around the ditch, broke and scattered, riders making off in every direction. Parties of cavalry fleeing away from the conflict meant one thing to units in the rear: defeat. The tension could have been broken by the exhilaration of making a positive attack, as it had been for the Allies. Royalist dispositions precluded that, and since they did not stand, tension for them broke in panic, and panic arose from disorder. In opting for the unconventional tactical decision, Rupert had hoped to bolster his numerically inferior cavalry. In opting for conventional response, Byron had thrown it all away.

'Our Horse and Foot with undaunted courage did put the Enemies right wing to flight, forcing them both from their Canon and Ammunition: (Ashe) . . . neither wearied by their former service, nor discouraged by the sight of that strength which the enemy [in centre and left] had unshaken and intire, but continuing and renuing their valour, they charged every party remaining in the field, till all were fully routed and put to flight: our men pursued the Enemies about three miles, till they came neere unto Yorke.' The Allies, wrote Cholmeley,[9] 'kept close together in firm bodies', not falling prey to the inevitable desire to pursue a broken enemy and thus to lose all cohesion. This restraint was very probably a concerted tactical decision reached by Cromwell and Leslie prior to battle, by which they intended to use their massive weight in numbers to best effect. However, as has been suggested, the very circumstances of the battle assisted in this plan not a little. Good commanders need luck as much as their own shrewd judgements. Having broken Byron's first line, the Allied cavalry had their impetus slowed down both by that action, and by the need to negotiate the ditch and then to reform. This enabled the commanders to control their men more easily. This stop to their headlong advance was emphasised by the resistance offered by Molyneux, and Cromwell's return to the field to take full charge probably contributed to the continuing ease with which his men were kept in hand. In comparison, Goring's headlong charge on the Royalist left wing (see Chapter 5) encountered no such pressures to slow down, and consequently speed precluded tighter control. Moreover, Cromwell was acting in concert with the infantry on his immediate right (see Chapter 6), and that would only have been practicable with the cavalry restrained. Numerical superiority and discipline were unbeatable.

'Give glory, all the glory, to God,' wrote Cromwell to Valentine Walton on July 5th, 'God made them as stubble to our swords.' In this same letter, he informed Walton with a heartlessness more apparent than real: 'Sir, God hath taken away your eldest son by a cannon-shot. It brake his leg. We were necesitated to have it cut off, whereof he died.' Perhaps Cromwell, retiring to where the surgeons were to have his wound dressed, found the young man being attended to, victim of maybe two or so rounds of cannon fire sent up by the Royalists before Byron's charge. 'He said to us', Cromwell went on, 'one thing lay upon his spirit. I asked him, What that was? He told me it was, That God had not suffered him to be any more the executioner of His enemies.' Cromwell was told that when the wounded man fell, he bade his comrades open their ranks a little 'that he might see the rogues run'.

The question of Cromwell's absence from the field to have a wound dressed introduces a bitter and protracted debate concerning his precise role in the Allied victory. The nature of the argument about Cromwell's contribution was not, and is not, purely military. It was never simply a question of old soldiers arguing about the niceties of old campaigns. Oliver Cromwell's political enemies attacked his career at all points, and not least at that point – Marston Moor – where he first came to more than ordinary notice amongst his contemporaries. Cromwell was a political soldier, unlike Sir Thomas Fairfax, or, indeed, Rupert or Goring. In examining the nature of the criticisms levelled at Cromwell, we both appreciate the degree of animosity felt towards him by erstwhile political allies, and see also the significance of the part he played in the battle, in spite of denigration. Eye-witness reports do not support the carping criticism.

Criticisms of Cromwell in his lifetime did not go unanswered, although he himself observed a dignified silence on the matter. The defeated Royalists made no attempt to deny to their great adversary his part in their discomfiture, and that seems to be crucial. Rupert himself, though he might accord responsibility for the defeat to the inscrutable ways of fate (rather than pouring denunciations on Byron), never denied Cromwell was an instrument of that fate. Presbyterians hostile to the evasiveness of the Independents for whom Cromwell seemed to speak; politicians hostile to the trial and execution of Charles I; those Republicans who felt themselves betrayed by the Protectorship and the rule of the Major Generals; from these came the slanders against Cromwell. It was part and parcel of a more all-embracing attack on the man's character and standing. He was the champion of a powerful army who, to some, betrayed principles for personal power. It is not surprising that a major factor in his career should have been subjected to vitriolic attack.

'Lieutenant General Cromwell', wrote Denzil Holles,[12] 'had the impudence . . . to assume much of the honour to himself.' According to Holles, the real work of the day was carried out by David Leslie, Lawrence Crawford and Thomas Fairfax, 'my friend Cromwell had neither part nor lot in the business. For I have several times heard it from Crawford's own mouth that when the whole army at Marston Moor was in a fair possibility to be routed, and a great part of it running, he saw the body of horse of that Brigade standing still, and, to his seeming, doubtful which way to charge, backward or forward, when he came up to them in great passion.' Crawford, whose impetuosity was not dissimilar to that of Byron, was Major General of Foot in the army of the Eastern Association, and was both a political and religious Presbyterian as well as being a career soldier, all grounds on which he would be suspicious of Cromwell. Since Crawford was himself killed in 1645 at the siege of Hereford, it is plain that he made no active contribution to the criticism of Cromwell, but rather his alleged criticisms were taken up by others, later. If there is never smoke without fire, there must have been some grounds for the stories. According to Holles, Crawford, seeing the Allied left wing hesitant, rode up to them 'reviling them with the name of poltroons and cowards, and asked them if they would stand still and see the day lost? whereupon, Cromwell shewed himself, and in a pitiful voice said: "Major General, what shall I do?" Crawford, begging his superior officer's pardon, told Cromwell: "Sir, if you charge not all is lost." ' Cromwell, the story goes on, insisted that he was wounded 'his great wound being but a little burn in the neck by the accidental going off behind him of one of his soldier's pistols'. Sending Cromwell off the field to have that wound dressed, Crawford himself 'led them on'. Two obvious questions might be, why did Crawford abandon his infantry command, and why did not David Leslie, in Cromwell's rear, assume chief command, both as a cavalry

84

general and as Crawford's technical superior? Is it to be believed that cavalry would obey an infantry general? It is doubtful that Crawford could have kept the cavalry in hand, but to raise doubts about Holles' allegations is to credit them more than is their due.

Bowles, an early defender of Cromwell's reputation, acknowledged that he had, indeed, been wounded, but after the first charge by his cavalry which had broken Byron's front line. 'Though it was not very dangerous, being but a rake in the neck, yet the pistoll being discharged soe neare, that the powder hurt his face, and troubled his eyes . . . a better excuse for withdrawing (if he had done so, which yet he did not).' Lord Saye, in his 'Vindiciae Veritatis or The Scots Designe Discovered', published in 1654, supported Bowles who had written in 1646. Saye was not then, apparently, aware of the stories circulating in Crawford's name, or if he was, disregarded them in favour of concentrating upon a story that merely gave David Leslie full credit for victory. 'An infamous lye of Cromwell', Saye observed of the criticism, 'as that I think [Leslie] himself hath so much Honor in him, that he will give . . . the lye in it'. The story Saye was refuting alleged that Cromwell 'did not at all appear in the heat of the business, but having at first a little skar, kept off till the worst was passed'. Saye said flatly 'it is known that [Cromwell] charged in the head of those Regiments of Horse in my Lord Manchester's army, which Horse he commanded, and with those Regiments broke all the Regiments of the Enemies Army, first the Horse, and after that the Foot, and herein indeed was the good service which David Lesley did that day, with his little light Scotch nags . . . that when a Regiment of the Enemies was broken, he then fell in, and followed the chase' in mopping up Byron's front line when Cromwell's first wave crossed the ditch and regrouped beyond it. It is true that Cromwell himself referred in a slighting manner to Leslie's men as 'a few Scots in our rear' in his lettter of July 5th, but that was a private letter, his remark was technically accurate, and it is not apparent that he voiced any criticisms of those Scots subsequently.

Sir Hugh Cholmeley in his account of the battle, ascribed to Leslie merely an advisory capacity in the triumph of the Allied left wing. 'An experienced old soldier', as he was, it is likely that Cromwell would indeed have sought his advice, perhaps have deferred to it. Yet Cholmeley was quite adamant from all that he had heard, that the allied left was successful thanks to 'Cromwell and his horse'. There was not even a hint in what he wrote to suggest that Cromwell was lacking in resolution, or absent for very long, or that Leslie – let alone Crawford – assumed responsibility and did what was necessary for victory.

Douglas, a Scot, who was on the field and rode under Leslie, recorded that Cromwell 'charged verie weel' but that 'at the first charge he was lightlie hurt, went off, and came out againe' which, according to Douglas, gave Leslie the chance to manage the Allied left temporarily and 'did good service'. This moderate Scottish view may be compared with that given by Somerville, after political divisions had contributed to a less than objective view of events: 'much of the victory is attributed to the good conduct of David Leslie. . . . Cromwell himself . . . distained not to take orders from him, albeit then in the same quality of command for parliament . . . whom, with the assistance of Scots horse . . . routed the prince's right wing'. Saye's view of Leslie's role, alluded to earlier, went on that by 'doing execution upon the [Royalists] and keeping them from rallying again and getting into Bodies', Leslie permitted 'Cromwell with his regiments . . . the better means and opportunity keeping firm together in Bodies, to fall upon the other Regiments which remained'.

An objective reconstruction of Cromwell's personal experience in the battle would seem to be as follows. Before the battle he and Leslie conferred together on tactics, and decided that if all went well and they managed to force the cross ditch and regroup – which from sheer weight of numbers was likely – they would endeavour to keep their cavalry in formation. This is supported by Cholmeley. Neither Cromwell nor Leslie could have foreseen that Byron would overturn his obviously defensive position in their favour. In the course of the hand to hand fighting after the overthrow of Byron's front line, Cromwell was wounded in one way or another – family tradition ascribes the deed to the sword of Marcus Trevor – and was obliged to fall back to have his wound dressed. It may well have been then that he came upon Valentine Walton's son being likewise attended to. It would not necessarily have meant that he quit the field altogether. In his absence, Leslie co-operating with Crawford (see Chapter 6) held the Allied line steady as it came into contact with Molyneux, and reinforced it with reserve forces crossing the ditch in more orderly manner. Cromwell, returning to the scene, assumed command again, and led the sweep across the field which finally routed the rest of the Royalist right, Leslie mopping up in his rear. The evidence for the co-ordination of the Allied left wing and the infantry on their immediate right strongly suggests the presence of a directing hand, and that would only have been Cromwell's. The story propagated by Holles and said to have come from Crawford, was – whether Holles invented it or believed it – a myth.

Once the Royalist right had been broken, and no counter-attack threatened, Cromwell with his 4,000 or so cavalry was free to direct them where he would. The failure of the musketeers under Napier to do their work must have cut down on the number of casualties Cromwell might have expected to sustain, so he cannot have lost very many men, although many would have been wounded in the fight with Molyneux. It is interesting also to note that the majority of known casualties sustained by the Royalists fell in the centre of the field or on their left wing, wherever the Royalists stood their ground unflinchingly, and that fact serves to underline the disintegration of the Royalist right.

Cromwell's initial triumph was crucial to the outcome of the battle, for he was able, with his strong cavalry well in hand, to move across the battlefield taking the enemy in flank and rear, undermining their resolve. The Eastern Association cavalry would not have responded to Leslie or to Fairfax in the way in which they responded to their own commander, and as further evidence is considered it will be apparent that much of the honour won by the Allies on July 2nd 1644 is rightfully Cromwell's.

NOTES

1. Carlyle, T., ed: *Oliver Cromwell's Letters and Speeches*, 1902 edn., Vol. I, p. 188.
2. Thomas Napier was a professional soldier who, in 1643, had come over from service in Ireland with his regiment, to join the King. See, *Calendar of State Papers, Domestic Series* 1661/2, p. 29.
3. Marcus Trevor, of 'Brynkinallt', Denbighshire, and of Rosstrevor in Northern Ireland, was an experienced soldier. Created Viscount Dungannon in the Irish peerage in 1662, he died in 1706.
4. John Lord Byron, of Newstead in Nottinghamshire, had been elevated to the peerage in December 1643 when he assumed supreme command in North Wales and Lancashire from Arthur Lord Capel. Byron died in exile in 1652.
5. Sir William Vaughan was a professional soldier with Irish experience, who like Napier had arrived in England in 1643. Styled by the Parliamentarians 'The Devil of Shrawardine' because of his activities on the Welsh border 1644/5, he was killed in Ireland in 1649.
6. Thomas Leveson was a native of Wolverhampton, and at this date was Governor of Dudley Castle. He died in exile in 1652.

7.   Thomas Maclellan, 2nd Baron Kirkcudbright (d. 1647) was not a soldier of any experience nor, as Young, in his work, has pointed out, was his regiment officered by professionals. Turner's remarks on the Scottish army will be remembered. Alexander Lindsey, Earl of Balcarres, was to have an undistinguished record in action against Montrose in Scotland, see Williams, R., *Montrose, Cavalier in Mourning*, 1975.

8.   Clark, J. S., ed: *Life of James II*, 1816, Vol. I, p. 22.

9.   Fuller, T., *Worthies of England*, 1811, Vol. II, p. 536.

10.   See Ross, W. G., 'Military Engineering During the Civil War', *Professional Papers of the Corps of Royal Engineers*, Occasional Papers, Vol. XIII, 1887, p. 129. Contemporary measurement was in geometric paces. I am grateful to Mr. Arthur Credland for discussion, and to Mr. John Knapton for correspondence, on these points.

11.   I am grateful to Dr. Keith Manchester M.B., B.S., B.Sc (Hons), F.R.A.I., for clarification on this subject. Attention should be drawn to Dr. Manchester's original contribution to an aspect of civil war casualties, 'Paleopathology of a Royalist Garrison', in OSSA, Journal of the Osteological Research Laboratory, Stockholm, Vol. 5, 1979.

12.   Holles, Denzil, *Memoirs*, 1699, p. 16.

Chapter 5

BATTLE 2:
'SUCH A CAVALIER-LIKE ASSAULT'

It has been shown that Lord Byron turned against himself the very advantages of terrain and of infantry deployment which ought to have safeguarded him. On the Royalist left, however, the terrain features so remarked upon by eye-witnesses as hazards to Sir Thomas Fairfax were fully exploited by Goring. When the Earl of Leven gave the signal for the general Allied advance, it was necessary for the Allied cavalry of the right wing and for the infantry to their immediate left to negotiate a very serious natural and man-made obstacle. This obstacle was a bank crowned with a hedge which marked the point at which the cultivated ground on which the allies stood met the moorland lying several feet lower. To tackle this hazard, it was necessary for Fairfax to pass his cavalry along a narrow lane and then to deploy them at the point where that lane debouched onto the moorland. All this had to be attempted in the teeth of concentrated musketry and under the sword's point of the Northern Horse there drawn up to receive them. The Royalist left had no single body of musketeers comparable to Napier's on the right wing, but there were bodies of musketeers interspersed amongst the sections of the cavalry as on the right. The obstacle at Atterwith Lane was far more serious for the Allied cavalry under Fairfax than for the infantry on his left, but when that cavalry was thrown back, the infantry flank was left exposed.

The array of the opposing forces in the Atterwith Lane area can only partially be reconstructed from the de Gomme plan and from that of Lumsden. The front line of the Allied right, commanded by Sir Thomas Fairfax himself, consisted of his horse drawn up in five bodies with blocks of musketeers between them. The second line, under John Lambert, was in four blocks, and the third or reserve line, commanded by the Scottish Earl of Eglinton[1] consisted of the regiments of, from left to right, Balgonie, the earl, and Dalhousie.[2] Some 4,000 strong,

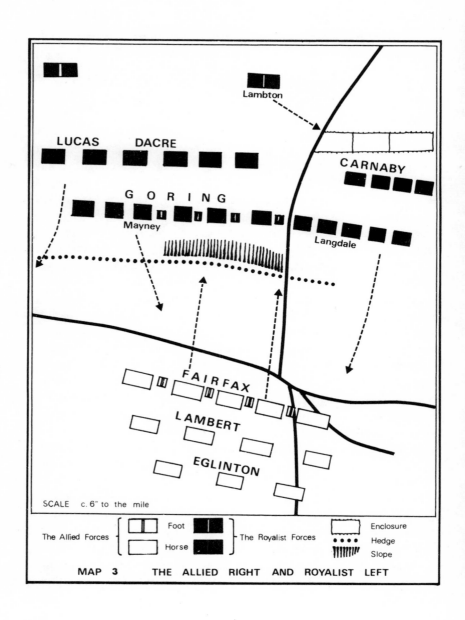

LUCAS   DACRE

LAMBTON

CARNABY

G O R I N G

Mayney

Langdale

FAIRFAX

LAMBERT

EGLINTON

SCALE c. 6" to the mile

The Allied Forces { ▭❘❘ Foot ■❘ } The Royalist Forces   ▭ Enclosure
                  { ▭ Horse ■ }   •••• Hedge
                                                          ⅏ Slope

MAP 3   THE ALLIED RIGHT AND ROYALIST LEFT

numerically inferior to the cavalry on the Allied left, they were also a mixed bag. On his return from Lancashire and Cheshire in late March, Sir Thomas Fairfax had brought with him some Lancashire cavalry units which cannot be said to have blooded themselves in any serious engagement for at least a year, if at all. Fairfax's own Yorkshire regiments had, of course, been involved in the long hard campaigns of 1643, had confronted Goring and his cavalry in the pitched fight on Adwalton Moor in that year and had gone on to success in Cheshire in early 1644. These Yorkshire regiments were, on the whole, veterans of at least twelve months' standing. Eglinton's Scots were an unknown quantity, but were in the event to prove themselves.

The Northern Horse on the Royalist left were better generalled than their comrades on the Royalist right. George Goring may have been a drunkard off the field, and the flamboyance of his manner may have aroused the animosity of civilian Royalists, but on the field he was a shrewd judge of his enemy's weaknesses. To support him he had the hard professionals, Sir Charles Lucas and Sir Marmaduke Langdale, whilst every regimental commander on the Royalist left, with the possible exceptions of Rowland Eyre and John Frescheville, had a year or more of campaigning experience to their credit. In depicting their precise array prior to battle, however, de Gomme's plan is not entirely reliable. Peter Young, who first perceived this, put forward a conjectural reconstruction placing Langdale in command of the extreme left of Goring's front line. In view of the fact that de Gomme indicated the position of Eyre and Frescheville to Langdale's immediate right in that line, and since neither of these officers was fitted to brigade command, in all probability it was here that Sir John Mayney exercised his rank of brigadier. Goring was with this front line, as Byron was with his, but whether with Langdale or Mayney is hard to say. To Langdale's rear and somewhat to his left, almost in a position analogous to Tuke's on the Royalist right, were the squadrons commanded by Colonel Francis Carnaby.[3] These were drawn up in the open fields of Long Marston village, and to the south of the Hatterwith enclosures, with intention both of guarding Langdale's flank and of supporting him in a charge. Immediately to the rear of Mayney, and somewhat to his right, were the divisions commanded by Lucas and Colonel Sir Richard Dacre,[4] acting both as a reserve but also, as we will see, as an independent formation. Further to the rear still lay perhaps two sections

91

of the York infantry, newly arrived from that city and not yet into line, whose role in the battle is dealt with elsewhere (see Chapter 6). These dispositions are set out on Map 3. In all, including the musketeers with which Goring had interspersed his cavalry, the Royalist left probably consisted of about 2,500 men, a numerical inferiority more than made up for by advantageous use of terrain, and further offset by the fact that they were virtually all battle hardened veterans. The same was true of Byron's cavalry, of course, but the crucial difference here was Goring's superior personal skills as a commander. Nevertheless, the small numbers of Goring's horse should be borne in mind in view of what was eventually to happen on that eastern edge of the battlefield.

'The right wing of Horse was intrusted to Sir Thomas Fairfax,' wrote Stewart, 'it did consist of his whole cavalry, and three Regiments of the Scottish horse, commanded by the Earl of Dalhousie, Earl of Eglinton, and Lord Balgony.' Sir Thomas Fairfax, wrote Lumsden, 'commandit thair in cheiff, ane brave commander, but his horse answered not our expectatioun, nor his worth'. Sir Thomas Fairfax himself remembered, 'I had the Right Wing, with some Scotch Horse and Lancers for my Reserve. . . . Our Right Wing had not, all, so good success, by reason of the whins and ditches which we were to pass over before we could get to the Enemy, which put us in great disorder.' Given the Allied decision to advance and to give battle, Fairfax was obliged to make the best of very poor circumstances, and Captain Stewart was very precise indeed as to what befell the Allied right. 'Betwixt them and the enemy there was no passage but at a narrow lane, where they could not march above 3 or 4 in front, upon the one side of the Lane was a Ditch, and on the other an Hedge, both whereof were lined with Musketiers', probably the skirmishers pushed forward earlier in the day when the Royalists had to consolidate their position on the moorland. 'Notwithstanding', Stewart went on, Sir Thomas 'charged gallantly, but the enemy, keeping themselves in a body, and receiving them by threes and foures as they marched out of the Lane, and (what mistake I know not) Sir Thomas Fairfax his new leavied regiment being in the Van, they wheeled about and being hotly pursued by the enemy, came back upon the Lord Fairfax Foot, and the reserve of the Scottish foot, broke them wholly and trod the most part of them underfoot.'

So complex was the action in the area of the Atterwith Lane that, before considering the experiences of the opposing forces, a summary of events is essential. It should be pointed out that since Fairfax had had at least twelve hours in which to deploy his cavalry, it is unlikely that his 'new leavied regiment' was in his van by 'mistake'. It is probable that Fairfax, given the terrain problem, and aware that any advance would involve his wing in fairly heavy initial losses, chose to commit a raw formation to bear that brunt of first contact with the enemy. Veteran cavalry, bringing up the rear could thus hope to deploy and consolidate on the moorland under cover of forces which might be expected to break anyway, but would offer a temporary respite for the veterans. As it turned out, the position was so terrible that even veteran cavalry broke, and all tactical considerations were of necessity banished from Fairfax's mind. The sequence of events was this: the signal for attack being given, the Allied right moved forward in conjunction with the rest of the army. Goring held his ground. Fairfax attempted to negotiate the ground between him and his enemy. Musketeers along the lane and beyond the bank opened fire when the Allies came within range. Fairfax and Lambert, commanding the first and second lines respectively, attempted to force their way onto the moorland, but their foremost troops were shattered by musketry fire, and rolled back onto those following them. A few sections of the Allied cavalry did manage to break through, but in no coherent formation, and simply strove to pass through the Royalists and reach the comparative safety of the open moorland further north. The Royalists, having received the attack and broken it, counter-attacked, the forces under Mayney, Langdale, Carnaby and probably Dacre, with Goring in command, sweeping up towards the ridge line. In his preliminary plans, Goring may well have allowed for this eventuality, and determined not to commit his entire cavalry to such a sustained counter-attack. Thus he left behind him a substantial body of horse under Lucas. Goring and his men, converging on the ridge line, encountered some resistance from Eglinton's reserve. The Scots for a time stood their ground, much as Molyneux stood his ground against Cromwell on the other side of the field. Breaking under pressure, the earl's cavalry wheeled about in flight, and were pursued by Goring's now largely unrestrained cavalry. Back on the moor, the collapse of Fairfax's wing had exposed the right flank of the Allied infantry centre, and against this Sir Charles Lucas, probably according to plan, turned his cavalry, with some unco-ordinated assistance from cavalry units to the rear of the Royalist centre (see Chapter 6). For a time, therefore, with the flight of the Royalist right and of the Allied right, fighting on the moor proper involved the infantry of the two armies, whilst shreds of Fairfax's cavalry made their way round to establish contact with Cromwell. The latter, circling the battlefield to the north and moving in unison with Lawrence Crawford's infantry, began to make his approaches to the Atterwith Lane area which would cause him to virtually occupy the ground held by Goring before battle was joined. Coming under fire from his left, from the Hatterwith enclosure, Cromwell was forced to turn his attention on these musketeers. During this temporary obstruction, Goring on the ridge line had opportunity to perceive his danger and to rally what cavalry he could to resist Cromwell. Finding the Hatterwith enclosure too tough a nut to crack, and in danger of losing momentum by preoccupation with it, Cromwell detached Fraser's Dragoons and David Leslie to finish it off, and pushed on. The Eastern Association cavalry now came into contact with such part of Goring's horse as had been kept together or rallied. For the second time in perhaps two hours, the Atterwith Lane area was the scene of a bloody encounter as Cromwell bent the power of his own cavalry against the fragmented and numerically inferior forces under Goring. This action was the deciding factor in the Allied victory.

Sombre evidence of the disaster which befell Fairfax's cavalry at the junction of the arable and moorlands may be adduced to support the emphasis placed by Stewart on terrain. When, in the mid 1960's, the bank which had used to mark off the arable from the common was levelled, leaving the gentle slope visible today, hundreds upon hundreds of musket balls were dislodged. These had embedded themselves in the face of the bank as a result of the concentrated musketry fire delivered from the Royalist left against the advancing Allies. The density of the distribution of this musket shot conveys very clearly the terrible impact on the Allied van when it rode into 500 musketeers firing, reloading, and firing again within a range of perhaps 70 to 100 yards. Precise figures for Allied casualties will never be achieved, but it is clear that at the Atterwith Lane hundreds of Allied cavalry must have been killed and wounded within a matter of a few minutes before ever Goring counter-attacked and added his charging cavalry to the panic spreading in Allied ranks. Charles Fairfax, Sir Thomas's brother, was mortally wounded, and Lambert's regimental major sustained 30 wounds. Small wonder, then, that Goring's cavalry were carried away by their sweeping success and gave themselves over to the furious delights of the chase. None of them knew that a formidable enemy would soon be gathering his strength in their rear.

'On the right wing,' wrote Arthur Trevor, 'we had infinitely the better of the enemy; so that in truth the battle was very doubtful.' Grifen noted 'the field went very dangerous in our right wing, for there [we] were routed, and many ran'. Sir Thomas Fairfax was, wrote Lumsden, 'ane brave commander, but his horse answered not our expectatioun, nor his worth'. Stewart stated that the Allied right, broken and turned back by their opponents, overrode their own foot in their desperation to be away, which must mean both those pockets of musketeers interspersed amongst them, and also a section of the Allied infantry centre. Lumsden stated that some of the discomfited cavalry under Fairfax blamed their 'commandit musqueteris' for failing to perform their part in the attack, but such criticism was probably obligatory. It is reminiscent of the grumbles about Hurry which certain Royalists made. Sir Thomas Fairfax's own recollection of events, whilst tending to underplay contributory factors such as the use of raw troops as a forlorn hope, is valuable, 'I drew up a body of 400 Horse. But because of the intervals of [Royalist] Horse . . . were lined with Musketeers which did us much hurt with their shot: I was necessitated to charge them. We were a long time engaged with one another; but at last we routed that part of their Wing. We charged and pursued them a good way towards York. Myself only returned presently, to get to the men I left behind me. But that part of the Enemy which stood, perceiving the disorder they were in, had charged and routed them, before I could get to them. So that good success we had at first was eclipsed much by this bad conclusion.' Fairfax here indirectly supports the sources which have the Scottish reserve line standing their ground, but when it comes to 'that good success we had at first', it is hard to square that observation with the reality. If Fairfax felt justifiably pleased that out of the wreckage of his wing he extricated a few troops of veterans and was then able to fight his way through the Royalist lines and so make safety, all well and good. Yet he had demonstrably failed to achieve anything else, and it is possible that when Goring counter-attacked the Royalists quite willingly opened their ranks to let Fairfax and his few men through, believing them to be no threat, as indeed they were not. These Allied cavalry, having thus passed through Goring's ranks, might have joined in the pursuit of the Royalist right wing. Sir Thomas himself, however, claimed to have ridden back alone towards the Atterwith Lane, taking the 'signal out of my hat' so that he might pass for a Royalist officer. Finding his cavalry had practically ceased to exist as a coherent force, and no longer possessing a command, by using his 'disguise' he eventually made contact with Cromwell who was circling the moor.

Captain Stewart was far more precise than Fairfax himself in explaining what had happened. 'Sir Thomas . . . Colonell Lambert and [Sir Charles Fairfax] with five or six Troopes charged through the enemy and went to the left wing of Horse [i.e., to find Cromwell], the two, Squadrons of Balgonies regiment being divided by the enemy each from the other, one of them being Lanceirs charged a regiment of the enemies Foot, and put them wholly to the rout, and after joined with the left wing of Horse [i.e., Cromwell] the other by another way also went to the left wing'. According to Stewart, therefore, Fairfax endeavoured to locate Cromwell immediately, and the precise nature of Stewart's reference to the lancers disposing of an isolated body of Royalist foot might square with Sir Thomas's less precise account of a pursuit. However, it should be pointed out that Bowles, a non-eyewitness, also wrote of 'good success' by Fairfax and Lambert, but went into no details. Both Stockdale and Ashe made no reference whatsoever to anything having been achieved by Fairfax, and both were in the field. Stockdale stated that 'many of our horse were . . . repulsed by the enemy', which remark allows for some breaking through, 'which coming of in disorder on all sides did soe daunt the spiritts of the reserves that had not then engaged as that many fled away. . . . I verily believe there were not so few as 4,000 of our horse that runne off the field.' Clarke, not an eye-witness, recounted that Goring 'rowted all the Lancasheire forces, and caused the Scottish horse to reatreate, and had the better of it'. Lionel Watson was even more explicit, and again an eye-witness: 'the enemies left Wing . . . wholly carrying the Field before them, utterly routing all our Horse and Foot, so that there was not a man left standing before them, most of the Horse and Foot of that wing . . . retreating', and causing, also, part of the Allied centre to fall back once their flank was exposed. W.H. writing of the Royalists, observed 'Their brave Chivalry in the left wing gave such a Cavalier-like assault that presently they routed our right wing, consisting of my Lord Fairfaxes men made up with some regiments of commanded Scots, who by the help of good horses ran so farre before they lookt about.' The severity of the action is implicit in Sir Thomas Fairfax's remark that 'many of my officers and soldiers were hurt and slain. . . . And scarce any officer which was in this charge, which did not receive a hurt.'

Thus, after risking a hazardous frontal assault and being broken up by the Royalist musketeers, a section of the Allied cavalry, 'but 5 troops', wrote Fairfax himself, after 'the business was hotly disputed a long time, at sword's point', broke through or were allowed through and made their way to the Allied left wing. They were subsequently followed by sections of Balgonie's cavalry including lancers. Now the Royalists were into their counter-attack. 'General Goring', wrote Cholmeley, 'who commanded . . . did with the northern horse charge the enemy's right wing so fiercely and home, as that he made the three generals . . . quit the field.' This was the point at which Leven, Lord Fairfax and apparently the Earl of Manchester, were caught up in the panic of their right and were either swept away in flight or even led the way. Nevertheless, the Royalist counter-attack was not entirely smooth going. Eglinton at least stood his ground at some point, probably in the immediate vicinity of the Long Marston/Tockwith road junction with the Atterwith Lane. 'My Lord Eglintoun commandit our horse there who shew himself weill, his son releiving his father who was far engaged is evill wounded.' Sir Thomas Fairfax himself did not give the Scots their due, a lapse of memory somewhat reminiscent of Cromwell's private slighting remark about David Leslie's Scots. But on the Allied right, as on their left, the Scots did not merely follow the flow of battle and do nothing else. Clarke's report that Goring 'caused the Scottish horse to retreate' does not correspond with his allusion to the rout of the other cavalry, and this fits with Douglas who spoke of his fellow countrymen standing firm 'till they were disordered'. 'The Earle of Eglinton's regiment maintained their ground', wrote Stewart, until they were driven off.

Establishing even a tentative time scale for actions on the field once battle had begun is difficult. If the Allied army advanced all its sections with initial precision (which is likely), then the disruption of Byron's Royalist right by Cromwell must have coincided with the horrific failure of Fairfax's line to take the moor and deploy. How long it was before Goring launched the charge that took his forces up towards the ridge line and beyond, is impossible to say, but if Fairfax after breaking through rode off to try to find Cromwell, he must have had some indication from the view of fleeing Royalist cavalry to the north of Cromwell's apparent success. In other words, Fairfax rode after Cromwell to find help not to offer any, for he had none to offer worth speaking of. It would seem then that while Goring dealt with Eglinton, Cromwell was dealing with Molyneux, and the time consumed by pursuit of the fleeing Allied right may have been equivalent to that occupied by Cromwell in circling the moor and swinging down towards the Atterwith Lane.

When Goring's cavalry swept forward, Sir Charles Lucas was detached to come in upon the Allied infantry flank exposed by the disintegration of Fairfax's cavalry, and henceforth Lucas's actions belong more properly to a study of the centre of the field (see Chapter 6). Quite suddenly, therefore, the area of the Royalist positions on the eve of battle, around Atterwith Lane, was emptied of anything beyond wounded men and perhaps stray groups of musketeers moving off towards the ridge in the wake of their cavalry. Only the Hatterwith enclosures with their York infantry remained occupied. Colonel Sir Philip Monckton[5] remembered: 'At the battle of Hessy Moor I had my horse shot under me as I caracoled at the head of the body I commanded, and so near the enemy that I could not be mounted again, but charged on foot, and beat Sir Hugh Bethell's regiment of horse, who was wounded and dismounted and my servant brought me his horse. When I was mounted again the wind driving the smoke so as I could not see what was become of the body I commanded, which went in pursuit of the enemy.' The fact that his own regiment left him behind and went off in pursuit shows to what degree the Royalist cavalry were carried away by their success so far.

How much anyone could actually see on the battlefield, as dusk gathered and with the thick, acrid smoke of ten thousand muskets drifting in whatever wind there was, is hard to say. One can picture Monckton standing in his stirrups and straining his eyes to ascertain the condition of the field in general. There was, for the moment, nothing for an isloated officer and his servant to do, and it is a pity that Monkton did not go into any detail concerning what he observed during a period of enforced inaction. That his regiment and the rest of Goring's cavalry had chased off the Allied right '& pursu'd y^m over ye Hill' (Slingsby) is supported by Allied accounts. 'The enemy being in pursuit and chase of

98

retreating men, followed them to our Carriages, but had slain few of them, for indeed they ran away before the enemy charged them', wrote Watson. The Royalist cavalry wrote Stockdale, 'possess themselves first of our Ordinance, and shortly after our carryages also which they first plundered, though afterwards it is conceived they were plundered by our owne Armeys, and some of the enemyes horse pursued our flying horse near two myles from the field, soe that in all appearance the day was lost'.

'Goring was possessed of many of their ordnance, and if his men had been kept close together as did Crumwell's, and not dispersed themselves in pursuit, in all probability it had come to a drawn battle at worst . . . but Goring's men were much scattered and dispersed in pursuit before they could know of the defeat of the Princes right wing' (Cholmeley). Ogden reported in his letter 'the left wing or horse made amends killed many of the enemyes, and charged through to Lesley's carriage and plundered it'.

Goring's numbers had dwindled: he might rally those busy rifling the enemy baggage, which doubtless stood where it had been when at 9:00 in the morning Leven had ordered his army back to the ridge, but he could not hope to call back those sections caught up in the exhilaration of the chase. Lucas, in the centre of the field, was spent (see Chapter 6). If Goring could count on 1,000 men now he was fortunate. Whether he saw the new threat with his own eyes from somewhere in the region of the Clump, or whether word was brought to him by a straggler coming out of the smoke and darkness gathering below, is not known. Perhaps the flashes of musketry from the Hatterwith enclosure drew his attention, and he sent a rider off to see what was happening. However it was, Goring was made aware that Oliver Cromwell, with 4,000 cavalry elated by success, and held intact ready to be unleashed again, was advancing towards him. All that Goring's men had done, had now to be done again.

The Eastern Association cavalry, reinforced by Lambert, Fairfax and Balgonie, skirting the centre of the field and supported by at least some of the Eastern Association infantry which, under Crawford, had been with Cromwell's cavalry since battle began, were homing in on the Atterwith Lane. 'Just then', wrote Watson, 'came our Horse and Foot from the chase of their right wing and seeing the business not well in our right, came in a very good order to a second charge with all the enemies

99

Horse and Foot that had disordered our right wing and main battell. And here came the business of the day.' Watson was, of course, right: and in his perception of the importance of the engagement about to ensue, provided further justification, if it were needed, that Cromwell was the instrument of Allied victory. 'The enemy's left wing', wrote Ludlow, 'who had been conquerors, returned to their former ground, presuming upon an entire victory; and utterly ignorant of what had befallen Prince Rupert but before they could put themselves into any order, they were charged and entirely defeated. . . .'

Leaving Fraser's Dragoons and some Scottish cavalry to deal with the Hatterwith enclosures, Cromwell and his main body 'stood in the same ground and with the same Front which they [the Royalists] had when they began the charge'. It was ironic that after utilising terrain to such a fine degree, Goring should now find himself, if he must dispute the matter, in the predicament in which Sir Thomas Fairfax had been broken. Watson was explicit: 'The enemy seeing us to come in such a gallant posture . . . left all thoughts of pursuit, and began to thinke that they must fight again for that victory which they thought had been already got. They marching down the Hill upon us, from our Carriages, so that they fought upon the same ground, and with the same Front that our right wing had before stood to receive their charge.' The long, steep incline of the flattened fields of crops on the ridge, the dirt road running parallel to it to be crossed, the trampled cultivated land and the narrow lane debouching onto the moor, the steep bank and an enemy waiting, this was almost a re-enactment of the scene earlier. It might be thought somewhat irrelevant to suggest, as was suggested, that had Goring kept his cavalry intact, things might have been different. Cholmeley insisted that a drawn battle 'at worst' would have resulted, implying that Cromwell, faced with an intact Royalist left, would have declined to offer battle. That is improbable, for he had the scent of victory and numerical superiority of at least two to one. Given that a struggle between Cromwell and Goring was inevitable, Goring was faced with two tactical alternatives, at least in theory. He might either have deployed on the moorland and launched a charge whilst Cromwell was partly occupied with the Hatterwith enclosures, or he might have deployed on the ridge and have Cromwell come to him. What seems to have happened is that Goring achieved neither, either because he was too slow in drawing men together, or because Cromwell moved too fast.

100

It looks as if Goring was caught in that same hazardous predicament which had ruined Fairfax.

The slaughter of the Royalists in this second engagement on the Atterwith Lane must have been considerable. Those forces at Goring's disposal did not flee the field, despite being outnumbered and faced with obstacles to their deployment. Watson linked the disposal of Goring's remaining horse to the final disintegration of the Royalist infantry, noting that 'Our three Brigades of Foot of the Earle of Manchester's being on our right hand on we went with great resolution, charging them so home, one while their Horse, and then again their Foot.' It was, all in all, a well executed manoeuvre by Cromwell.

What part Sir Thomas Fairfax played in this second engagement is unclear, but he exercised no actual command. He himself did not suggest other than that he rode as a plain cavalryman. The action was Cromwell's, David Leslie being detached first to the Hatterwith enclosures, and then to fall in upon the Royalist infantry of the centre before coming in on Goring's cavalry flank. The fighting may well have gone on well after dark, given the determination of Goring's men, indeed of the Marquess of Newcastle's army as a whole, to stand their ground. Colonel Sir Richard Dacre was mortally wounded here, and later rumour claimed that Sir Marmaduke Langdale had been taken prisoner. The cavalry regiment of William Eure,[6] a veteran force which had seen action both in the south of England and with Newcastle, sustained a savage assault if the deaths of Eure and of his Lt.-Colonel, Henry Topham of Aglethorpe in Yorkshire, may be considered a guide. Sir Henry Slingsby's nephew, Colonel John Fenwick,[7] was also killed. Francis Salvin of Croxdale, Co. Durham, Major in the cavalry regiment of Sir Richard Tempest, was killed, and many others. Bodies on seventeenth-century battlefields did not normally lie in heaps, unless they were gathered up for burial, but the ground at the bank and foot of the narrow lane was thick with wounded, dead and dying, Allies of the first action, Royalists of the second, mingled together.

The Royalist officer casualties are direct evidence of the bitterness of this action. For how long it lasted, whether the Royalists gave ground steadily or were thoroughly overwhelmed, the sources are silent. Goring and his commanders – those not killed or taken prisoner – escaped to York under cover of the deepening darkness, no doubt riding through Long Marston village street or flat out across the open fields in the general direction of the city. Cromwell's men could now relax, some going off in pursuit, but the majority probably too exhausted to do other than dismount and collapse on the moor. On the ridge, however, Colonel Sir Philip Monckton, not apparently caught up in Goring's defeat, had an experience that serves to indicate how fragmented the Royalist cavalry had become. 'I retired over the Glen', he wrote, 'where I saw a body of some two thousand horse that were broken.' Whether Monckton's assessment of their strength was particularly accurate or not is beside the point. It was a substantial body of Royalist cavalry. Where did they come from? The Northern Horse, 4,000 strong when they approached York on June 30th, had been somewhat dispersed on the battlefield. Goring had the bulk, but the commands of Sir Edward Widdrington and of Sir William Blakiston (see Chapter 6) had been posted in rear of the Royalist infantry centre. Monckton was not the only writer to mention that body of 2,000 inactive near the Glen. Somerville wrote of 2,000 intact in the general vicinity of the eastern end of the battlefield, and Cholmeley, Ashe and Watson all recounted that 2,000 or so Royalist horse had entered York on July 1st. However, given the nature of the fighting and what had befallen Byron's right wing, it is likely that the cavalry with whom Monckton came into contact were a composite grouping of already spent troopers. 'As I endeavoured to rally' them, wrote Monckton, hoping to attempt something upon the weary Eastern Association cavalry, 'I saw Sir John Hurry . . . come galloping through the glen. I rid to him and told him, that there was none in that great body of horse but they knew either himself or me, and that if he would help me to put them in order, we might regain the field. He told me, broken horse would not fight, and galloped from me towards York. I returned to that body. By that time it was night and [Sir Marmaduke Langdale] having had those bodies he commanded broken, came to me, and we staid in the field until twelve o'clock at night, when Sir John Hurry came, by order of the Prince, to command me to retire to York.'

The only way in which Hurry could have appeared in the glen would have been for him to have passed clean through Cromwell's and Leslie's cavalry in the fight on the Royalist right, in much the same way as Sir Thomas Fairfax passed through Goring's men. Both found themselves in rear of the enemy. That the 'broken' horse would know both Monckton, a north country commander, and Hurry, suggests that this body was made up of elements of several broken formations: primarily, those which had set off in pursuit of the Allied right wing and returned to the field too late to fight with Goring, or unwilling to commit themselves to a useless struggle; secondly, elements of the Royalist right which, like Hurry, had been left behind in Cromwell's sweep across the field; and thirdly, of what was left of Lucas's and Blakiston's cavalry (see Chapter 6) which remained in the vicinity. A further element may have been made up of cavalry come late from York, bearing in mind what Cholmeley, Ashe and Watson said. That this motley body of cavalry stayed, without firm leadership, in the battlefield from the commencement of the fighting to at least midnight, indicates the extreme degree of disorganisation during the battle. They cannot have been so 'broken' as Monckton claims Hurry called them, and it will be noted that they were ordered to retire, and waited for those orders. However, it is one thing to be aware of their presence, and another to follow Monckton's inference that he might have used them to save the day. The battle was ended. The Allies were probably scattered and weary, but the Eastern Association, however exhausted, had kept its cavalry intact and was too formidable to be challenged. Cromwell had won the battle of Marston Moor.

Royalist defeat can be traced directly to the failure of John Lord Byron to stand his ground on the Royalist right. Had he obeyed orders, had he permitted Cromwell to face the full rigours of the reception Rupert had arranged for him, the outcome of the battle would have been entirely different. Goring's triumph over Fairfax bore no relation to anything happening elsewhere on the field. Given that almost inevitable success and given Byron's ability at least to disrupt the Eastern Association cavalry and to fend them off until Rupert arrived with reinforcements, then the break-up of the Allied army as their centre lost its cover on its right flank, would have been beyond prevention. From the moment that Byron transgressed, the Royalists had begun to lose, for it does not seem that it would have been possible for Goring, heavily outnumbered, to check Cromwell's cavalry, and, as events turned out, he did not. Goring and his commanders did their best in a situation virtually thrust upon them by a Royalist general.

The Northern Horse, at the least, did make an attempt to reverse the inevitable. Yet if any action of either side on Marston Moor demands an astonished admiration, then it must be that self-sacrificing stand made by a body of the Marquess of Newcastle's infantry, and to a consideration of the infantry fighting we must now turn.

NOTES

1. Alexander Montgomery, 6th Earl of Eglinton, was now in his 56th year. He went over to the Royalists in 1649, was imprisoned by Cromwell, and died in 1661.
2. Lord Balgonie or Barlgony had been wounded in action on 19th February at Corbridge during the invasion, and commanded the Earl of Leven's own regiment of horse. William Ramsey 1st Earl of Dalhousie went over the Charles II in 1651, and died in 1674.
3. Francis Carnaby was of Togston, Co. Durham, and was probably about 24 years of age. He was killed in October 1645 riding with the Northern Horse.
4. Colonel Sir Richard Dacre is assumed to have been of the family of Dacre of Lanercost, Cumberland, but extant pedigrees are silent concerning him. He was knighted in the field by the Marquess of Newcastle.
5. Sir Philip Monckton was 22, of Cavill, Yorkshire, and was a devoted Royalist until the restoration, from which point he developed a resentment at the way in which former enemies of Charles I were favoured, which led him into serious trouble with the government. See Peacock, E., ed: *The Monckton Papers*, Philobiblon Society, 1884.
6. Colonel Eure was 41, a younger son of William 4th Lord Eure, of Old Malton, Yorkshire, and a Roman Catholic.
7. John Fenwick of Hexham, Northumberland, was 32, and had been MP for Morpeth in the Long Parliament. His father, Sir John Fenwick of Wallington, went over to the Parliament in late 1644.

Chapter 6

BATTLE 3:
'OUR FOOT PLAYD THE MAN'

Writing on July 5th, a correspondent of Sir Philip Musgrave, the Royalist Colonel General of Cumberland and Westmorland, sending him news of the battle, observed: 'Our losse is mostly in Comaunders and ye foot, my Ld Newcastle had in Yorke', and added 'Our foot playd the man, but the horse jades'. This was somewhat unkind in view of the performance of Goring's cavalry on the Royalist left wing, yet, in the allusion to the gallantry of the Royalist foot, the writer acknowledged the stubborn resistance shown by those infantry, and most particularly, by the Marquess of Newcastle's own regiment. The fate of that regiment, commanded by Sir William Lambton, although it occurred in rear of the Royalist left wing of horse, is part and parcel of the experience of the Royalist infantry in general. Although their position on the field was somewhat isolated, it cannot be treated in isolation.

Infantry deprived of the support and protection of cavalry on its flanks, and coming under renewed pressure from enemy infantry and from enemy cavalry, cannot of itself either win a battle or force a draw. Foot under such circumstances, however hard they might fight, have in reality three choices. They might attempt to flee the field, in disorder, dodging parties of enemy cavalry mopping up stragglers. They might surrender, undergo a few days enforced idleness and want of rations, and then be released on their paroles not to bear arms again. They might, finally and very rarely, resist the offer of quarter and the chance of surrender, and elect to fight on and to die. It is one of the remarkable features of Marston Moor that one Royalist regiment, a regiment of repute and of proven valour, chose, when all was clearly lost, to refuse the offer of quarter made to them by an admiring enemy, and to die in rank and file. Their action salvaged not a little honour from a battle where such honour as there was clearly belonged to Cromwell's cavalry. Such cases of defiance were few during the civil wars, and often

105

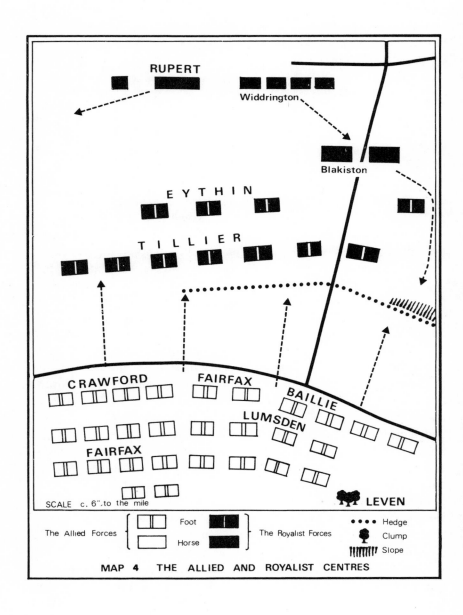

MAP 4   THE ALLIED AND ROYALIST CENTRES

occurred where there was really very little choice in the matter: the defenders of Basing House in Hampshire, for example, and the Royalist outlaws caught up in the vicious massacre perpetrated by Cromwell at Drogheda in Ireland. Although a parallel might be drawn with the defiance of the Cornish foot at Lansdowne in 1643, the position of the Whitecoat regiment on Marston Moor was unique in that nothing was to be gained by their resistance, and quarter was, indeed, offered them.

Stewart, Douglas, Ashe, Watson and Lumsden provided sufficient detail of the dispositions of the infantry in the Allied centre to allow a fairly detailed reconstruction of their position when battle was joined. There were, in all, some 11,000 Allied infantry drawn up in Marston Fields, excluding the musketeers commanded off to operate with the cavalry of either wing. The forward line of the Allied foot was deployed in eight main divisions forming the left and right of the centre, and two divisions of Lord Fairfax's Yorkshire foot drawn up between them and forming the middle section of the infantry centre (see Map 4). Behind this forward line was a second composed of eight divisions, and to the rear of this was a third of similar size, with apparently a further two divisions making a reserve or fourth line. It was a very dense array, but in its regimental constructions indicative of the speed with which it had been formed by Leven during the earlier part of the day, hurriedly putting regiments into line as they marched back to the ridge. The Allied positioning concealed a fundamental weakness inherent in the dispersal of tried and raw regiments, so that Manchester's Eastern Asociation infantry were split into two very unequal parts, and the Yorkshire infantry under Fairfax were similarly divided. This was not a mistake made on the cavalry wings, which had had all day to arrange themselves to their best advantage.

Major General Lawrence Crawford (see Chapter 4) commanded the four divisions of the Eastern Association foot on the left of the centre's forward line, with Cromwell's cavalry to his left. Drawn up in his rear in a second line were the Scottish regiments of Yester, Livingstone, Coupar and Dunfermline[1] from left to right respectively. The third line of the Allied centre left was composed of four divisions of Lord Fairfax's infantry, and behind these were two further Scottish units. Two divisions of Lord Fairfax's foot composed the centre of the Allied front line, with Crawford on their left. Drawn up behind them were the Scottish regiments of Kilhead and Cassillis,[2] and in a third line behind these, the Scottish regiments of Erskine and Dudhope.[3] The front line forming the right of the Allied centre had four Scottish regiments, those of, from left to right, Rae, Hamilton, Maitland and Crawford-Lindsay.[4] The centre right was, however, poorly supported. From all the evidence it seems that neither Maitland nor Crawford-Lindsay had any support whatever, the regiments of Buccleugh and Loudon[5] in a second line supporting Rae and Hamilton only, and themselves supported by a third line composed of two divisions of Manchester's Eastern Association foot. This weakness of the extreme centre right was to prove problematical for the Allies when battle was joined. The Scottish foot in centre and centre right were commanded by Major General Sir James Lumsden, whose account is one of the authorities for the battle, while Lt. General William Baillie[6] commanded the Allied front line of the centre right. It ought also to be noted that the three generals, Leven, Manchester and Lord Fairfax, were present in the infantry centre, although whether enjoying any active field command themselves is uncertain. Sir Alexander Hamilton, an outstanding soldier, commanded the Scottish Artillery.

The strength of the Royalist centre ought, if all had been well, to have been roughly equal to that of their opponents, perhaps a few hundred less. In point of fact, Rupert cannot have had more than 9,000 or 9,500 foot deployed. It was not a staggering numerical inferiority, and need not have mattered given the stability of their flanks: but what it betokened was a scattering of infantry elsewhere on the moor which, acting entirely without co-ordination, contributed nothing to the effective prosecution of the battle and was, as in the case of those foot scattered by Balgony's lancers, taken out piecemeal. This was what happened to Lambton's regiment. It has been shown that de Gomme's plan of the Royalist dispositions may be considered inadequate as a guide to the precise position of the York infantry forces. From after 9:00 am until 4:00 pm Rupert's own infantry had kept the centre of their army, thinly strung out and waiting for the York foot to fall into line behind them. As it turned out, only a part of the York foot managed to achieve this before battle began, so that it is probable that some movement of Royalist infantry occurred after the de Gomme plan was drafted, as a response to changing circumstances. We can assume then that the front line of the Royalist foot as given by de Gomme and shown on Map 4 was that which, with some unrecorded alterations, prevailed when battle was joined. This front line, commanded by the professional soldier Major General Henry Tillier, like Napier in Ireland until late in 1643, consisted of (from Royalist right to left) the regiments of Warren,[7] Tyldesley (who was with his cavalry regiment on the Royalist right wing), Broughton,[8] Earnley and Gibson[9] and that of Tillier himself. Warren's regiment was flanked to its right by the cavalry regiment of Marcus Trevor, and Tillier's had on its left the Brigade of Sir John Mayney. Immediately to the rear of the front line, forming part of an intended second line, were, from right to left, the regiments of Chaytor[10] (technically a northern regiment. but picked up by Rupert en route to York, somewhere in the West Riding), Millward and Chisenall.[11] This allowed for the York foot to fill the gap in the second line, behind the regiments of Warren and Tyldesley. Map 4 indicates that this second line was commanded by Eythin. It is probable that when battle did begin, Eythin had about 1,500 of the York foot in a body, roughly in that intended position, but the rest were strung out across the moor.

A curious feature of the deployment of the Royalist army in the centre is the positioning of two cavalry brigades in rear of the infantry. These were commanded by Sir Edward Widdrington and Sir William Blakiston.[12] Widdrington's, well to the rear and positioned close to the westward arm of the tracks which met at Four Lanes Meet, deployed to the left of Prince Rupert's Lifeguard (which indicates where Rupert himself was much of the day), and was intended as a reserve, to be sent to either wing as necessity required. However, Blakiston's was drawn up to the rear and left of the infantry under Millward and Chisenall, and can only have been thus deployed to support the foot until the York reinforcements should arrive. Very probably, this brigade would then either have fallen back to join Widdrington's, or have shifted over to the Atterwith Lane to be with Goring. When battle began, however, Blakiston was still carrying out this covering role, and his strength was spent in an unco-ordinate charge which, once broken, deprived him of any further effective part in the battle.

Arthur Trevor, who met Rupert and his officers within a day of the battle, stated that the Allied advance began when the York infantry appeared on the field. That observation is crucial. From the ridge line, Leven and his fellow generals could see the precise location of all the Royalist foot, and would in particular have noted the inevitable dislocation of the York infantry regiments debouching from the lane from Hessay and being hurriedly brought into position. It was an ideal moment to launch a general advance. The Allied generals could regard the isolated York contingents as more or less out of the reckoning, and it was almost certainly not until Cromwell's cavalry came under flanking fire from the Hatterwith enclosures, that it was evident that Lambton's, at least, although isolated, was not harmless.

Infantry regiments were, ideally, 1100 strong, although most commanders of the civil war thought themselves lucky if they could muster half that strength. Each regiment consisted of two musketeers to every pikeman, and the ratio was probably maintained even when the regiment was at half strength. The musketeers, the effectiveness of whose weapons has been discussed (see Chapter 4), were the 'common herd' of a regiment, it being considered more gentlemanly to carry the pike. The first shock of battle in the centre of the field would entail musketery fire, pikemen acting as cover to the musketeers at close quarters, or against cavalry assault. The two basic methods of infantry action were 'introduction' and 'extraduction'. In the first, after the front rank of musketeers had given fire, the second rank advanced before them and did the same, and so on, making a steady advance. In the second, the front rank having fired, would fall back to the rear and the second rank, then giving fire, would do the same. This allowed for orderly retreat. There were variations. The musketeers, for example, deployed in three ranks, might fire as one, the rearmost rank standing, the second stooping and the front rank kneeling, which gave a more concentrated volley. Under attack from cavalry, well-trained regiments could form two concentric rings, musketeers on the outside, pikemen on the inside, when the length of the pike came into its own. Sometimes as much as 18 feet long, 15 feet of which would be the wooden stave, the pike, tipped with a steel spike, served in the capacity of a primitive bayonet, the development of the bayonet proper obviating the need for pikemen and making the 'common herd' of musketeers the norm.

Infantry field officers – colonels, lt.-colonels and majors – would attend to their duties from horseback, and it was therefore rare for an infantry commander, unless he dismounted or was unlucky, to be killed or taken prisoner. He had the means of escape if all went badly. Sir William Lambton, in the Hatterwith enclosure, dismounted and stood with his men, which, as will be seen, was probably crucial to their resolve, and certainly led to Lambton's death.

110

The sequence of events in the centre was as follows. When the signal to advance was given, the Allied infantry moved forward in order. Crawford, left of centre, with no obstacle before him, made good time, assisted in clearing Napier's foot from the cross ditch hindering Cromwell's cavalry, and came into contact with Warren's and probably with Tyldesley's, having turned their flank somewhat. Lord Fairfax's foot to Crawford's right penetrated the hedge before the Royalist position and drove back the soldiers under Broughton. The Scottish foot on the Allied centre right came into contact with Earnly, Gibson and Tillier, and were held. Now, the success of the Eastern Association cavalry permitted Cromwell and Crawford to work in conjunction to turn the Royalist flank, while on the other wing the collapse of Thomas Fairfax's cavalry meant that the regiments of Maitland and Crawford-Lindsay, lacking support, and brought to a stand by Tillier, had their flank exposed as well. Lord Fairfax's foot, having driven back Broughton, found him strengthened by some York infantry, and were themselves driven back. At this point, Blakiston's cavalry from their position in rear of the Royalist centre, charged down on the retreating regiments of Fairfax's foot and on those of Hamilton and Rae next to them. This assault was followed up by a second cavalry assault on the exposed Allied flank by Sir Charles Lucas, detached from the Royalist left wing and endeavouring to complete the destruction of the enemy centre. But Maitland and Crawford-Lindsay stood firm, and Lucas was held off. After Blakiston's charge, petering out on the ridge line, his cavalry were assailed by Eastern Association foot and driven back onto the moorland where they were broken up. As for Lucas, unable to end the resistance of Maitland and Crawford-Lindsay, in a third charge he was himself dismounted and taken prisoner, and his brigade was spent. The suddenness of the Allied collapse on their right wing, and Blakiston's initial success caused Leven, Lord Fairfax and Manchester to take to their heels followed by their soldiers, but Lumsden, Hamilton and Lawrence Crawford stood firm. Sound re-deployment of infantry saved the Allied centre.

The Eastern Association cavalry, with Crawford's infantry on their right, now swung steadily east under Cromwell, folding up the Royalist centre which had lost all cavalry support. Widdrington's brigade, held in reserve by Rupert, had probably already been swallowed up in the flight of Byron's wing. In the manoeuvre, the Eastern Association cavalry came under fire from Lambton's musketeers in the enclosures and, after leaving Fraser and Leslie to deal with them, rode on to rout Goring (see Chapter 5). It was now a business of mopping up, accepting surrender, and dispersing such formations of Royalists which still seemed disposed to fight. But without the success of Cromwell's manoeuvres, assisted by Crawford's foot, such a situation could not have been brought about and until Rupert's wing was entirely broken, the battle in the centre was very much in balance.

'The main bodies joyning, made such a noise with shot and clamour of shouts that we lost our eares and the smoke of powder was so thick that we saw no light but what proceeded from the mouth of gunnes', wrote W.H., vividly depicting his experience of black powder warfare. The rival infantry, each regiment made up of two musketeers for every pikeman, exploded into life with a crash of gunfire. For the Allied attackers, it was at first smooth going, in that they obtained a general success in forcing back the Royalists opposed to them. However, this was not maintained. While Lawrence Crawford and the Eastern Association foot managed to maintain their advance with the help of Cromwell's cavalry uncovering the right flank of the Royalist centre, Lord Fairfax's foot and the Scottish foot of the centre right ran into trouble.

'Upon the advancing of the Earle of Manchester's foot', wrote Ashe, 'after short firing on both sides, wee caused the enemy to quit the hedge in a disorderly manner', thus assisting Fraser's dragoons in routing Napier at the cross ditch, and also breaking the resistance of Warren's foot. 'General Major Crawford having overwinged the enemy set upon their flank and did very good execution' (Stewart). 'In a moment we were passed the ditch into the Moore', remembered Watson, 'upon equall grounds . . . our men going in a running march.' Manchester's foot 'did good service' conceded Lumsden, who was himself preoccupied with the centre right where the initial advance had come to a standstill and some degree of panic was spreading as circumstances on the Allied right wing changed. Part of Crawford's success lay in the fact, as pointed out by Stewart, that there was nothing in the way of an obstacle between him and the Royalists to negotiate, the cross ditch itself positioned in such a way that it could be taken in flank without actually being crossed by the infantry. From henceforth, Crawford and the Eastern Association cavalry worked together: 'Our foot on the right hand of us', wrote Watson, '(being only the Earle of Manchester's Foot) went on by our side, dispersing the enemies foot almost as fast as they charged them still going by our side, cutting them down that we carried the whole field before us.'

Watson was describing a tactical manoeuvre that could only have been carried through by infantry and cavalry used to working together, and it was part of the strength of the Allied army that where it mattered, on the left wing, Eastern Association horse and foot stood side by side.

The collapse of the Royalist right and of the Allied right led to exposure of the flanks of the opposing infantry. On the Royalist right of centre, however, the collapse was more spectacular if Crawford's success is any guide, whereas on the Allied right of centre the Scottish regiments, although in a similar position, held firm even under cavalry assault. The solution to this apparent contradiction must lie in the availability of reserves. There were no troops that could be rushed to bolster Warren's foot, whilst Lumsden, seeing the critical situation with Maitland and Crawford-Lindsay, was able to shift forces rapidly across the field to support them and thus save that section from collapse.

Rupert, it will be remembered, when battle began so unexpectedly, was at supper in rear of the Royalist centre, accompanied by his Lifeguard of Horse and with Widdrington's brigade close at hand. First he rallied his own regiment of horse, and joining these with his Lifeguard, Rupert led them into an attack intended to support Molyneux, who was holding his own on the right wing. The success of the Cromwell-Crawford manoeuvre depended upon the breaking of that right wing, and it is improbable that Widdrington's brigade was involved in Rupert's counter-attack. It is even likely that it was that brigade which Newcastle endeavoured to halt, it being composed of his own cavalry. From the moment that Byron's line broke, Widdrington's was crucial, and yet it was swept away in panic. Failing to rectify the situation on the right, Prince Rupert 'being separated from his troope [i.e. Lifeguard] and surrounded by the enemy, killed 4 or 5 wth his owne hands, and at last hee brake strangely through them'. Rupert's failure to repair the damage to his cavalry and their utter rout in consequence gave Cromwell and Crawford the chance to liaise, although Ogden, who wrote the foregoing, also insisted that Crawford had not had it quite so smoothly as other sources strongly imply: '[Rupert's foot] suffered much, they standing soe stoutly to it, and the horse flying: most of

113

Manchester's blew coats wch fought under the bloody colours are cutt off' (i.e. killed). Nevertheless, the aid given by Cromwell's cavalry greatly facilitated Crawford's movements, and then the aid became mutual. The failure of Sir Thomas Fairfax on the Allied right in much the same way hazarded the infantry of Lord Fairfax and Baillie.

'The Lord Fairfax his brigade . . . did also beate off the enemy from the hedges before them, driving them from their Canon, being two Drakes and one Demi-culvering', wrote Ashe. 'The Battell was led on by General Hamilton, Lieutenant-Generall Baylie . . . the Reserve being committed to the trust of Major-General Lumsdaine', wrote Stewart, and he went on: 'Upon the advance of our Battell' the Royalists (in this case, Earnly's, Gibson's and Tillier's) were 'forced to give ground', the Allied infantry clearing the hedge and that westward section of the bank which at Atterwith Lane was so steep, but which was more gradual a drop near Moor Lane. Stockdale noted Lord Fairfax's foot gaining 'ground of the enemyes foot in the maine battle'. W.H. stressed that it was 'hotly disputed between the two main bodies'.

After initially falling back, the Royalist infantry opposed to Hamilton and Baillie rallied, supported by elements of the York foot. They 'furiously assaulted' Fairfax's men, causing them to retreat 'in some disorder'. This must have coincided to some extent with the disintegration of Sir Thomas Fairfax's cavalry which, negotiating under fire the Atterwith Lane, finally broke and scattered, when it came into the full storm of musketry, and took off to right and to left. They 'came back upon the L. Fairfax Foot', wrote Stewart, and the reserve of 'the Scottish Foot, broke them wholly, and trod the most part of them under foot'. At this point, Sir William Blakiston, looking for an opportunity to employ his small cavalry force to effect, swung east around the flank of the Royalist infantry and led a charge against the now disordered Yorkshire and Scottish foot. 'They charged through them to the top of the hill' (Stewart). Douglas stated that 'Fairfax briggade of foot fled, the Edinburgh and artillerie regiment followed, first the Chancellor and Maclaines fled, some levie of all the horsemen of the enemy charged up where they were fleeing.' 'So disordered', wrote Stockdale, the Scots and Lord Fairfax's foot 'were forced to fly back and leave our Ordinance behind them . . . so that the enemy had the advantage to regaine their owne ordinance which my Lord Fairfax Brigade did first beat them from.'

The effectiveness of Blakiston's action was apparent but limited. He added to the enemy disarray, and appears to have kept his cavalry in hand once they reached the ridge top. However, what Blakiston's objective may have been after that charge is uncertain. It is probable that he saw the battle from the point of view solely of the Royalist left wing cavalry, or, in other words, was not aware of what had happened to the west. If so, his charge was simply a 'blooding' for his men in the general sweep towards almost certain victory. If that was so, it was probably only when he reached the ridge and looked about him that he perceived how black things were, supposing that the smoke and gathering darkness permitted full realisation. Clearly, Blakiston, no mean commander to judge by his later record, would have achieved more had he liaised with Lucas, or rallied to Rupert.

It was probably in the wake of Blakiston's own attack that the Marquess of Newcastle now saw action. It will be remembered that when the decision to postpone battle had been made at about 4:00 or so in the afternoon, he had retired to his coach, but was called from repose by the ominous rattle of gunfire signalling action. He 'immediately put on his arms, and was no sooner got on horseback, but he beheld a dismal sight', in the flight of part of the Royalist right wing, and perhaps of Widdrington's. Failing to rally them, the Marquess at first determined to locate his own regiment of foot, 'to see in what posture his regiment was' (the Duchess wrote). This would appear to mean that the Marquess was not clear as to Lambton's whereabouts which would be understandable in view of the situation in the Royalist lines. However, he was deflected from his purpose by the arrival of his Lifeguard under Sir Thomas Metham, and determining to charge south directly into the main fighting, Newcastle passed nowhere near his regiment which he would have done, had they been properly into line. Newcastle and his 'gentlemen volunteers' went on 'and passing through two bodies of foot, engaged with each other not at forty yards distance, received not the least hurt, although they fired quick upon each other; but marched towards a Scots regiment of foot which they charged and routed; in which encounter my Lord himself killed three'. This description sounds very much as if Newcastle, if not acting in consort with Blakiston, was nonetheless associated with the latter's charge, and it is not beyond possibility that Newcastle inspired the move, Blakiston being of Newcastle's army. He might even have driven them on away from the ruinous spectacle of the Royalist right in flight. 'At last, after they had passed through this regiment of foot, a pikeman made a stand to the whole troop' wielding his 18 foot pike until some got inside his guard and killed him. From this point, what happened to the Marquess is unknown, but we know that he kept the field well after all was lost.

In the wake of Blakiston's charge, the Royalist foot recovered their ground, but Blakiston's contribution was finished. On the ridge line, he halted and swung east, facing the now fleeing ranks of the Allied cavalry of their right wing. In this area was that part of the Eastern Association foot which was drawn up as part of the third line of the Allied infantry immediately in rear of the Scottish foot.

These foot now 'did wheele on the right hand upon their Flanck, and gave [Blakiston] so hot a charge, that they were forced to flie back disbanded into the Moore' (Ashe). Blakiston's now much disintegrated cavalry, returning whither they had come, conscious at last, probably, of the turn of events, collided with advance detachments of Eastern Association Horse circling the field to the north, and 'many of them were killed in the place, and about two hundred by the Scots Horse [i.e., David Leslie's] were taken prisoners'.

Blakiston's charge broke up further the cohesion of the Allied centre, and gave the Royalist foot a breathing space in which to reoccupy the ground they had previously been forced from, recapturing their guns. The degree of Allied collapse at this point is amply testified to by Lumsden: 'These that ran away shew themselffs most baselie. I commanding the battel was on the heid of [Loudon's] regiment and Buccleughes but they carryed not themselffs as I would have wissed, nather could I prevaill with them. For these that fled never came to chairge with the enemies, but wer so possessed with ane pannik fear that they ran for example to others and no enemie following, which gave the enemie occasion to chairge them. . . .' Yet, in much the same way as the Earl of Eglinton stood his ground when the cavalry of the Allied right broke up, so the regiments of Maitland and of Crawford-Lindsay now stood their ground though exposed on either flank, and to far better purpose, as it turned out, than Eglinton who was, at last, forced to retreat (see Chapter 5). 'They that faucht stood extraordinarie weill to it; whereof my Lord Lyndsay, his brigad commandit by himself, was one', wrote Lumsden. These regiments, until reinforced by Lumsden, held the full weight of an attempt by Sir Charles Lucas detached from

Goring's wing, to break their resistance.

The fight between Lucas's cavalry and the Scottish regiments was a classic of infantry-cavalry fighting. There was probably no co-ordinated musketry fire from the Scottish ranks, but the pikemen now came into their own. The front rank, the pike projected upward and its base secured against the inside of the right foot: the second rank, pikes held at waist height: and the third rank, pikes lifted above their heads, for thrusting downwards. Lucas 'assaulted the Scottish Foot upon their Flanks so that they had the [Royalist] Foot upon their front and the . . . Cavalry of the enemies left wing to fight with, whom they encountered with so much courage . . . that having interlined their Musquetiers with Pikemen they made the enemies Horse, notwithstanding for all the assistance they had of their foot, at two severall assaults to give ground: and in this hot dispute with both they continued almost an houre, still maintaining their ground' (Stewart). Lumsden and Baillie now drew up reinforcements to assist the two regiments thus showing their worth: 'These brigads that failyied on the vanne wer presently supplied by Cassilis, Kilheid, Cowper and Dumfermling and some of Cliddisdaills regiment who wer on the battel, and gained what they had lost, and maid themselffs masters of the cannon was nixt to them', Lumsden wrote. Stewart confirmed this, stating that Baillie and Lumsden 'perceiving the greatest weight of the battell to lye sore upon the Earl of Linsies, and Lord Maitelands regiment, sent up a reserve for their assistance, after which the enemies Horse having made a third assault upon them, had almost put them in some disorder'. On this third charge, Lucas's horse was killed under him – probably by a pike thrust – and he fell into enemy hands, dragged into the midst of the Scottish regimental formations. The repeated failure of the Royalists to force the pikes, and Lucas's capture, saved the flank. Now, the Scots began to gain ground against Tillier's foot.

If not quite the end of the battle, it was virtually that. 'Our foot . . . altho a great while they maintained yᵉ fight yet at last they were cut down & most part either taken or kill'd', wrote Slingsby. The routing of Goring's hitherto successful cavalry by the Eastern Association horse, with some assistance from David Leslie, and the movement of Crawford's foot around the field, completed the destruction in the centre. The battle was already lost to the Royalists, when the Whitecoat regiment went down.

While the term 'Whitecoats' might have been applicable to several of the foot regiments of the army of the Marquess of Newcastle, it is evident that only one of these was involved in the last stand described by the sources. In particular, Captain Camby told Lilly of 'this sole regiment', and Camby had been a trooper involved in trying to dislodge them. The Duchess of Newcastle[13] referred to the valour of her husband's own regiment of Whitecoats at the siege of York. They had been raised in North Durham and around Newcastle-upon-Tyne in the late summer of 1642 and, as Newcastle's own, such a force would have been a prestigious regiment to which to belong. Because of Newcastle's duties as Lord General, he followed normal practice in appointing a colonel to command his regiment, and this colonel was Sir William Lambton of Lambton Castle, Co. Durham.[14] Under Lambton, the regiment was one of the two chosen to force the passage of the River Tees at Piercebridge on December 1st 1642, a bloody action which saw the death of Lambton's fellow colonel, Thomas Howard of Durham. Further, at Wakefield in May 1643, when the battle was all but lost to the Royalists and the town fallen, it was this regiment alone which, offered quarter, 'scorned the motion' to surrender.[15] Known as the Whitecoats, like other regiments sharing that uniform, this regiment was also known as Newcastle's Lambs. The allusion here to their founder and to their colonel's surname and armorial bearing – Sable a fesse inter 3 lambs passant argent – will be obvious. This regiment carried Newcastle's regimental colours, and it was incumbent upon them to see that those colours were not stained with dishonour. From such sources for the northern army as we have, it is more than apparent that this regiment sustained very severe losses. In 1660, only six officers of varying rank were still certainly alive. This compares with no fewer than 17 from the Durham regiment of John Hilton[16] which also fought on Marston Moor, yet which was probably nowhere near Lambton's in strength.

Eythin brought 3,000 infantry to Marston Moor, roughly the equivalent of three infantry regiments at full strength. Since, however, few regiments in York garrison would have been at half strength, and probably at much less, this force from York may have been made up from six to ten regiments. Apart from Newcastle's own, which because of its prestige would probably have been the strongest, certainly the more easy to recruit, and Hilton's, the only other northern foot regiments which we can be sure were present on Marston Moor were those of Colonels Richard Tempest[17] and Sir Marmaduke Langdale. The others cannot certainly be identified, although Henry Chaytor's was, as has been said, technically northern. The only infantry commander to die on Marston Moor holding full colonel's rank, was Lambton. As has been said, infantry colonels were mounted, the better to attend to their duties, and so were able to escape a stricken field with as much ease as their cavalry counterparts. Lambton, therefore, probably dismounted in the enclosure as a gesture of solidarity with his men, a move fitted to time of crisis. Newcastle himself picked up a pike and charged with his infantry at Adwalton Moor in June 1643. The regiment in Hatterwith enclosure was a regiment of repute, with a tradition of resistance, and is the only northern infantry regiment which can be demonstrated to have lost heavy casualties in the civil war.

Cromwell and Leslie, wrote Somerville, met with no 'great resistance' until they 'came to the Marquis of Newcastle his battalion of white coats'. Lambton's men, utilising their sheltered position to try to alleviate the impact of the Eastern Association cavalry on the Royalist left, drew attention to themselves by opening fire upon Cromwell's lines of horse, 'first peppering them soundly with their shot' and, when Cromwell directed his cavalry against the enclosure to try to force Lambton's men to scatter, they 'stoutly bore them up with their pikes, that they could not enter to break them. Here the parliament horse received their greatest loss, and a stop for some time to their hoped-for victory, and that only by the stout resistance of this gallant battalion.'

The reasons for this resistance have been suggested in part. A veteran regiment, Newcastle's own, guardians of Newcastle's colours, found themselves isolated when battle began. Rather than flee, Lambton put them into the protection afforded by enclosures in rear of the Royalist left wing, and there they might have stayed virtually isolated but at least on the field and prepared for action. Perhaps Lambton hoped to stay there until contact was made with Newcastle himself, and retire under orders with no honour lost. It seems certain that the Marquess did not set eyes on his regiment at any time after he himself left York in the late morning. The evidence shows that he intended to join them, but was distracted by his Lifeguard and involved in the Blakiston charge. Once the Eastern Association cavalry swung to the east, there was no passage to the enclosure, even supposing

119

Newcastle himself did know where the regiment was. Lambton, his men under cover and held together, isolated from the battle, quite suddenly found the power of Cromwell's cavalry moving down in Goring's rear, and yet within musket shot of the enclosure. If he could not stop that advance, he might hinder it. He might give Goring time to regroup. There was still some hope. The Whitecoat regiment fired upon Cromwell's cavalry in flank.

'As good men as were in the world', wrote Cholmeley of them. Mrs. Thornton, one of many civilians who would have heard the story afterwards, wrote of them as 'the brave white coats foote that stood the last man till they were murthered and destroyed'. The Duchess, referring to this action, observed: 'His White Coats showed such an extraordinary valour and courage in that action, that they were killed in rank and file.'

It does look as if Lambton took upon himself and his men more than they could handle. Being who they were, they died rather than dishonour their colours.

Cromwell turned his strength against them. He could not shift them. If he dallied too long attempting it, his own losses would increase and Goring would rally and grow strong enough to meet him head on on the moor. On the other hand, Cromwell could not leave that regiment in his rear with safety. So he split his forces. He left a 'Scots regiment of dragoons, commanded by Colonel Frizeall [Fraser], with other two . . . to open them upon some hand, which at length they did; when all their ammunition was spent, having refused quarter, every man fell in the same order and rank wherein he had fought', concluded Somerville. Lilly prefaced his presentation of an eye-witness account by stating: 'A most memorable action happened that day.' The Whitecoats, the Lambs, within their ditched enclosure, 'by mere valour, for one whole hour, kept the troops of horse from entering among them at near push of pike. When the horse did enter, they would have no quarter, but fought it out till there was not thirty of them living; those whose hap it was to be beaten down upon the ground as the troopers came near them, though they could not rise for their wounds, yet were so desperate as to get either a pike or sword, or piece of them, and to gore the troopers' horses as they came over them, or passed by them.' The bitterness of this part of the fighting is clearly presented by Lilly, who was more than impressed by the information he had from Captain

Camby, 'then a trooper under Cromwell', and the allusion to wounded Whitecoats grasping at broken weapons to offer further resistance graphically illustrates the whole affair. Captain Camby, 'who was the third or fourth man that entered amongst them, protested he never in all the fights he was in, met with such resolute brave fellows, or whom he pitied so much, and said, "he saved two or three against their wills" '. Lambton was killed, Captain Samuel Kennet of Coxhoe, Durham, was killed with him, and Kennet's father wounded but saved. Of all the Whitecoats, only these three can be identified with any certainty.

David Leslie, after attending to the overthrow of the Lambs, turned his horse simultaneously against what was left of Tillier's infantry giving ground now in the immediate vicinity of Moor Lane, and against the flank of Goring's cavalry hard pressed by Cromwell. The area of Marston Moor between the open fields of Long Marston village bordering the Atterwith Lane, and the land just to the west of Moor Lane, was the area where the battle was won and lost. By the time that darkness fell, and Sir Philip Monckton (see Chapter 5) was busily trying to persuade Sir John Hurry to attempt something with some 'broken horse' in the glen, Cromwell's cavalry were sitting their horses in the midst of a great slaughter, and some were busy chasing the runaways toward York to prevent them from reforming. The silence that must then have fallen after so much clamour, punctuated as it was by the sounds of dying men and horses, must have been as fresh and cool as a wind blowing the powder smoke away.

'Wee have had a great fight', wrote Sir Philip Musgrave's correspondent on July 5th, 'where wee have got a defeat.' It was a quite staggering Allied victory, given the complete failure of the Allied right and the virtual collapse of the bulk of the Allied commanding generals. Sir Thomas Fairfax's cavalry had broken, and Sir William Blakiston in a tremendous charge had swept his way to the summit of the ridge to emphasise that all seemed lost. It was even said that Prince Rupert sent despatches early from the field to claim a victory, but that may well have been the merest nonsense, intended to stress the reversal of fortune which had befallen the Royalists thanks to God's favour and his chosen instrument, Cromwell. Lesser instruments of divine power, for the Allies, were Eglinton's horse, and the regiments of Maitland and Crawford-Lindsay, while Lawrence Crawford's infantry deserved their due.

The battle of Marston Moor was a series of more or less fragmented actions. Once the Royalist right wing was broken, Manchester's cavalry encountered no real resistance until they swung round to the Royalist left. The infantry action in the centre resolved itself into a bloody thrust of pike contest between Tillier's foot and the Scottish regiments. Blakiston conducted a charge with rewarding results, and yet had, in his isolation, been dispersed and broken despite it. The regiment of Sir William Lambton, however, exemplifies the unco-ordinated aspect of the field. Cut off and theoretically deprived of any value in the battle of massed ranks, that regiment resolved to stay on the field until it could decently withdraw. Suddenly, it found itself confronted with a developing situation which it might in some way interfere with, or at least help to reduce the pressure under which Goring would be coming. In an action entirely self-induced and thoroughly unrelated to the infantry action in general, Lambton's regiment which had come so late, showed the quality of Newcastle's infantry. Goring won a success, dissipated his strength, and then offered to resist Cromwell in a doomed action which saw the deaths of many commanders. When it was over, Goring and his cavalry escaped. Lucas, after vainly trying to break the hedgehog pikes of the Scottish infantry, fell captive and his horse dispersed. Monckton, up on the ridge, chafed and fretted and did nothing. Only Cromwell, moving across the darkening moorland like some bright-eyed beast of prey, seems to have seen the field as a whole and to have acted the part of a general. That his men and Lambton's fought it out between them is, in hindsight, appropriate. The power that was growing against the power that was ending, elite against elite.

NOTES

1.   John Lord Hay of Yester, created Earl of Tweeddale in 1646: Alexander Livingstone, later Earl of Calendar: James Lord Coupar: Charles Seton 2nd Earl of Dunfermline.
2.   The Douglas of Kilhead, 'whose cariage with his regiment hath beine nothing inferior to those of the best', wrote Leven in August. John Kennedy 6th Earl of Cassilis (died 1668).
3.   Colonel Sir Arthur Erskine. James Scrimgeour, 2nd Viscount Dudhope, died of wounds sustained in action against Blakiston's brigade.
4.   Colonel James Rae: General of the Artillery Sir Alexander Hamilton: John Maitland 2nd Earl of Lauderdale: John Lindsay Lord Lindsay of the Byres, Earl of Lindsay, ratified as 17th Earl of Crawford in 1644.

122

5. Walter Scott, Earl of Buccleugh. The Earl of Loudon was not present at Marston Moor, but his regiment was commanded by Lumsden. Loudon was recipient of Lumsden's written account and plan of the battle.

6. William Baillie went over to the Royalists in 1648 and served in the invasion of England in that year. He, Lumsden, Hamilton and Erskine were the most experienced commanders Leven had at his diposal.

7. Henry Warren of Burghclere, Hampshire, was a professional soldier who like Tillier and Napier, Earnley and Gibson, had come over from Ireland in 1643.

8. Robert Broughton of Marchwiell, Denbighshire, was a professional soldier with Irish experience.

9. Sir Michael Earnley, a professional soldier, died of the effects of wounds and terminal consumption in April 1645. Richard Gibson had been Major General of Foot under John Lord Byron in North Wales.

10. Henry Chaytor of Croft, Yorkshire, 'a brave and discreet officer', died in 1664.

11. Edward Chisenall of Chisenhall, Lancashire, was appointed a full colonel by Prince Rupert in June for his part in the defence of Lathom House in that county. A barrister, he died in 1653.

12. Sir William Blakiston of Archdeacon Newton, Co. Durham, was knighted in 1643. Second in command of the Northern Horse 1644/5.

13. Newcastle Memoir, p. 37.

14. Both the present writer and Brigadier Young, independently of each other, earlier concluded that Newcastle's colonel was Sir Arthur Basset of Umberleigh, Co. Devon. This judgement was based upon the interpretation of a source published in 1663, *A List of Officers Claiming to the Sixty Thousand Pounds Granted by his Majesty for the Relief of his Truly-Loyal and Indigent Party*. Basset certainly served under Newcastle, and was knighted by him, from some stage in 1643, but when Newcastle's regiment was formed in 1642, Basset was then in the West Country and there is no evidence to suggest that he joined Newcastle prior to 1643. Indeed, the only direct allusion to him in the north comes in early 1644, and this does not imply that he was connected with Newcastle's Whitecoats, whereas Lambton's case seems fairly strong.

15. Vicars, John, *Parliamentary Chronicles*, 1646, Vol. I, p. 338.

16. John Hilton of Hilton Castle, Co. Durham, Esquire, died in 1658.

17. Sir Richard Tempest, 3rd Baronet, of Stella, Co. Durham, was a cavalry commander in the 1648 rising. His major at Marston Moor was John Kennet, whose brother Samuel was killed in the Whitecoats and whose father was wounded there.

Chapter 7

AFTER MARSTON MOOR

Prince Rupert, escaping the field, arrived at York at 11:00 that night, where he either met or was joined by Lord Eythin. The Marquess of Newcastle 'being last in the field' of all the Royalist generals and 'seeing that all was lost' made his own way to the city and found Rupert and Eythin there waiting for him. Sir Charles Lucas, Henry Tillier and Commissary General George Porter were prisoners: Metham, commander of the Marquess's Lifeguard, was dead in the field. Sir Richard Dacre was conveyed to York, dying, and was buried in the city on July 18th. Sir William Wentworth, a gentleman volunteer, was buried at Poppleton, close to the point at which Rupert so early in the morning had crossed the bridge of boats to offer battle to a retreating and apparently demoralised enemy. The rout of the Royalist army should not, however, conceal the fact that the Allied army was itself disorganised and scattered. Arthur Trevor, who had gone to York to find Rupert, wrote, 'I could not meet the Prince until the battle was joined, and in the fire, smoke and confusion of the day, I knew not for my soul whither to incline. The runaways on both sides were so many, so breathless, so speechless . . . not a man of them being able to give me the least hope where the Prince was to be found; both armies being mingled, both horse and foot; no side keeping their own posts.' Trevor believed that it was only the fall of darkness which 'made cessation of arms' and gave the infantry opportunity to slip away. Ogden, with slight exaggeration, wrote that the Allies themselves 'had not after the fight 500 foote in a body'.

CASUALTIES

'The Enemies being all beaten out of the field', wrote Ashe, 'the Earle of Manchester, about eleven a clock that night, did ride about to the

124

Souldiers' praising them and assuring them of rations come the morning. Now began the grim business 'when the Bodies of the dead were stripped' by the Allied infantry. W.H. wrote that the truth was the Royalists 'behaved . . . with more valour and resolution than ever man saw coincident with so bad a cause'. The number of the dead, dying and wounded was horrific proof of that. 'The moone with her light helping something the darkness of the season' (Stockdale), facilitated the work in hand. Ashe initially believed that 'about three thousand of the Enemies were slaine; but the Countreymen (who were commanded to bury the Corpes) tell us they have buried foure thousand one hundred and fifty bodies'. Douglas, Stockdale, Watson all agreed with the estimate of the countrymen, but this figure reflects the number of those buried during the course of July 3rd and 4th. Shelley wrote of 'many more killed in ye pursute', and Watson referred graphically to the Allies following the chase of fugitives 'within a mile of Yorke, cutting them down so their dead bodies lay three miles in length. . . . I cannot think', he went on, 'but of all dead in the field, in the woods and mortally wounded (which would die within a day) there are between three and foure thousand' and more.

Alfred Burne believed, with reason, that the site of burials on a battlefield indicates the area of thickest fighting, but for Marston Moor there is no certainly identified burial area, despite what tradition claims. The area of the Atterwith Lane and between that and Moor Lane, was certainly, from all the evidence, the area of greatest slaughter. The heaviest Allied losses occurred here, when Fairfax tried to force the Royalist left wing, and when Cromwell and his cavalry came into range of the musketry of Lambton's men. Here also perished a large number of Goring's cavalry in that second cavalry action which marked the end of the battle, and likewise the 500 or 600 Whitecoats, perhaps more, in their narrow enclosure. It would therefore stand to reason that somewhere in that area a series of substantial mass graves would have been dug, but although there are stories in the locality of farm workers discovering human remains, these appear to relate to isolated graves, perhaps of persons overlooked in the earlier mass burials. Given that the countrymen of Hessay, Long Marston, Tockwith, Bilton, Wilstrop, Rufforth and Moor Monkton – the surrounding villages – did, like medieval heralds, number the dead as they buried them with some accuracy, those 4,150 interred in the day or so following the battle cannot be a final total. Sepsis setting in after musket wounds, the slower deaths of many wounded men in days and weeks to come, would push the number of fatalities directly attributable to Marston Moor far higher. It is a total that can never be established, but to suggest half as many again – at least 6,000 dead – would not be unreasonably high. For the Royalists, moreover, the death toll was doubly serious. Newcastle's foot had been shattered beyond recovery: a few of his infantry officers would continue to serve as volunteers, and many of them would die at battles somewhere else, Malpas, Ormskirk and Naseby. The real loss lay in the deaths of numerous veteran commanders: Dacre, Eure, Lambton, Fenwick, Sir Charles Slingsby, and hundreds of company and troop commanders. 'Captain Winget told me from an honest man that overlooked the dead', wrote Burgoyne, 'that amongst them all he thought there were two gentlemen to one ordinary soldier that was slain.' Douglas noted 'many private men' were killed, whilst the story of Sir Charles Lucas being taken over the field by his captors to identify gentlemen who might be removed for private burial is well known.

Wounds were not all physical, to be remedied by recovery or death. Thomas Goad, vicar of Grinton in Yorkshire, was a Royalist chaplain on the battlefield and after the battle fled to Doncaster 'fell ill and became distracted, in which condition he still remains', wrote a friend in 1660.[1] Some were lucky. Captain John Thomlinson of Thorgamby and Brayton in Yorkshire, a cavalry captain in the regiment of Newcastle's eldest son, Lord Mansfield, was 24 when he rode to Marston Moor. Shot between his legs, he was left for dead, but a day or so after the battle a lady travelling in her coach towards York saw him move, and conveyed him to the Allied siege lines where he received attention and recovered, dying in 1680.[2]

EQUIPMENT

Experienced commanders might be hard to replace, but the rank and file, given ordinary luck, can be replaced in time. Far harder to repair would have been the loss of equipment. 'Wee took all the Enemies Cannon, Ammunition, Waggons and Baggage', wrote Ashe. 'The Earle of Manchester hath for his part, ten pieces of Ordinance, one case of Drakes, foure thousand and five hundred Muskets, forty barrels of Powder, three tun of great and small bullet, eight hundred Pikes, besides Swords, Bandilleers. . . .' This was the Eastern Association's share of the spoils alone. Captain Stewart stated that 25 guns in all were captured, 'neere 130 barrels of Powder, besides what was blowne up by the common Souldiers, above an hundred Colours, and ten thousand Armes besides two Waggons of Carbines and Pistols of spare Armes'. Douglas and Stockdale reckoned the number of arms taken to be about 6,000 in all, but Stockdale acknowledged a report of 10,000 whilst Clarke, a secondary source, accounted for 14,000. The official Despatch, however, coming from the three generals who had access to all reports, opted for Stewart's 10,000 as the true figure. Shelley settled the point by alluding to 6,000 found 'in ye place, besides divers more cast into ye woods and hedges'. The Allied soldiers, when they had the leisure to look about them, picked the battlefield more or less clean, leaving only those weapons broken beyond reasonable hope of repair, and salvaging cannon balls as well where they could be found. Musket balls were not important, except in quantity, but all other items of equipment not trodden into the ground by the movement of men and thus hidden to the eye, would be retrieved and put to use. Only one sword, a pikeman's or musketeer's side-arm, which when lost was still in good shape, can with certainty be ascribed to the Marston Moor, and this was found over a hundred years ago. Soldiers of 17th-century armies, who of necessity lived a hand to mouth existence much of the time, would not be lax in the cleaning up of a battlefield, both of necessary equipment, and in stripping good, usable clothing from the corpses of friend and foe alike. War is a depressing business when momentary excitement subsides.

London propagandists, making much of Rupert's defeat, took delight in the discovery of Rupert's 'Sumpter-horse' which was found loose in Wilstrop Wood on July 3rd. Tracts were adorned with woodcuts of crucifixes, rosaries and other objects indicative of the Roman Catholic conspiracy which, with a monotony bordering upon distraction, they insisted lay at the root of the civil war. There were plenty of Catholic officers on the moor – Molyneux, Tyldesley, Leveson, Eure, Lambton, Tempest – and no doubt plenty of crucifixes to pick up, but Rupert was no Catholic. Delight was also taken in the discovery of the corpse of Rupert's pet poodle, Boy, which must clearly have gone everywhere with him. If the tracts did not go quite so far as to suggest that the poodle was a witch or demon in animal shape, they came close.

127

'At the dawning of the day' of July 3rd, wrote Cholmeley, 'there was rallied together two thousand horse who had great inclination to have acted something upon the prevailing party of the enemy's other wing, but that they were prevented by an order to retire to York.' This was Monckton's and Langdale's body of 'broken horse', for which Rupert had sent at about midnight. They mustered outside York, for the governor of the city, Sir Thomas Glemham, strict military man as he was, refused access to any but survivors of the original garrison. As July 3rd wore on, the runaways from the Royalist right wing drifted in, so that 'there are not now an hundred wanting' (Ogden). Somerville believed that given this accession of strength, 'if the prince having so great a body of horse entire, had made an onfall that night [i.e., during the darkness of July 2nd/3rd] or the ensuing morning betimes, he had carried the victory out of their hands; for it's certain, by the morning's light he had rallied a body of ten thousand men, whereof there was near three thousand gallant horse'. A pardonable exaggeration by a Scot who, like many of his fellow countrymen four years on, would begin to wonder if they ought to have won the battle of Marston Moor at all. On the morning of the 3rd, Cholmeley went on, 'the Prince had thoughts of a new supply of fresh foot out of York, to have attempted something upon the enemy but that he was dissuaded by General King, and though the enemy was much broken and dispersed and not possessed of the Princes cannon and baggage till the next morning'. The only 'fresh foot' in York were the regiments left behind in the city as a garrison, doubtless at Eythin's connivance, those of Sir Henry Slingsby, Henry Wait and what was left of John Belasyse's foot much damaged at Selby on April 11th. Eythin, who all along had warned against depleting the York garrison on the chance of beating so formidable an army as that of the Allies in the field, no doubt did dissuade the Prince from this scheme.

The precise nature of the confrontation at York in the early hours of July 3rd is not known, nor that it was, as it well might have been, a confrontation. Rupert had every cause in the world to blame Eythin for a large part of the defeat, and that he did indeed do so is evidenced by a letter which Eythin wrote to Rupert in January 1645 from Hamburg: stating that he was suffering the effects of a 'multiteud of grieffs', he said that he had been informed when he was on his way into exile on July 4th

you should heave sent to steay me and to recall me bak and that by reason
of som tratourous act Yr Highnes had to leay to my cheardge[3]

It was certain that Eythin was not guilty of treachery. Yet, in view of a
very grave dereliction of duty, it is surprising that Rupert did not
endeavour to bring Eythin to account, and Eythin's belated letter may
be the outward indication of a guilty consciousness of what he had done.
For, after more or less sabotaging Rupert's tactics on July 2nd, on July
3rd he patently interfered with attempts to repair the damage.

At the meeting on July 3rd, according to the Diary, Eythin asked
Rupert what he would now do. 'Sayes ye P I will rally my men. Sayes
Gen$\underline{^{ll}}$ King [k]now you w^t Ld Newcastle will do? Sayes Ld Newcastle I will
go into Holland [looking upon all as lost]. The P would have him
endeavour to recruit his forces.' This at least confirms what Cholmeley
had to say. 'He and the Marquess having once agreed that the Marquess
should go to Newcastle, whither the Prince would return as soon as he
could recruit his foot; which if it had accordingly been pursued had been
of great advantage to the King's affairs, for had the Marquess remained
in those parts surely a great number of the broken foot would have
rallied together, and it would have given encouragement to the King's
friends.' However, Cholmeley stated, Eythin, 'considering the King's
affairs absolutely destroyed by loss of this battle persuaded the
Marquess (against all the power of his other friends) to quit the
kingdome'. The story that Prince Rupert, when faced with this decision,
tore 'my Lo^d Newcastle's commision before his face'[4] can be dismissed.
The Prince accepted the idea of exile as a temporary expedient, and put
Newcastle's authority into commision, sharing it between Sir Thomas
Glemham and George Goring.[5] The Marquess's exile involved not only
his immediate family and entourage, but also the bulk of his northern
army general staff. Eythin was to go with him, William Lord
Widdrington the President of his Council of War, Sir William Carnaby
his Treasurer at War (whose younger brother, Colonel Francis Carnaby,
also opted to leave), Sir Francis Mackworth, infantry major-general,
and half a dozen or so other officers. It was a general staff that, to all
intents and purposes, had lost its army. Prince Rupert, by his superior
authority, kept the Northern Horse with him, and Goring, Langdale
and Mayney were willing enough to follow the prince. There were no
foot regiments left of which to speak, and as Eythin must have pointed
out to Newcastle, it was pointless to exercise a general's authority when

there was nothing over which to exercise it. It is not really surprising that Newcastle abandoned the idea of trying to recruit afresh. He was despondent and defeated.

YORK ABANDONED

Either late on July 3rd or early in the morning of Thursday July 4th, Newcastle left York. As his escort rode Colonel Sir John Mayney with a detachment of the Northern Horse. Their first stop was Scarborough, where Sir Hugh Cholmeley was governor and much of whose information concerning events was gathered from his important guests over two days sojourn in the castle. Meanwhile a ship was prepared in Scarborough harbour, and on July 7th the exiles sailed for Europe. 'There was diverse other gentlemen of' Yorkshire 'who desired to pass at the same time, but the governor would not permit them, it being as he conceived prejudicial to the King's affairs', Cholmeley wrote.

This was the first and not unimportant result of the battle fought on July 2nd. The northern army had ceased to exist, such parts of it as remained intact either isolated in garrisons or electing to stay with Rupert. In York, Glemham was obliged to make what terms he could for the surrender of the city, the garrison of which must have been severely demoralised by the defeat and by the depletion of the soldiery which had done duty so well between April and the end of June. 'Thus were we left at York', wrote Slingsby, 'out of all hope of relief, ye town much distract'd, & every one ready to abandon her'. To placate the discontent, Glemham gave out false reports that Rupert, who had marched away on July 4th, 'had fallen upon ye enemy suddenly & rout'd y^m, & that he was coming back again'. Within a few days this was seen to be patently untrue. 'Ye enemy taking a few days respite to bury their dead, to provide for ye wound'd, & to gather up such scatter'd troops of foot & horse as had left ye feild . . . were now in readiness to march back again to York.' Leven sent a summons for the surrender of York on July 4th, which Glemham rejected, whilst at the same time sending a letter after Rupert urging him to remember the plight of the city.[6] On the 11th, Glemham consented to a parley, commissioners were appointed by both sides, and terms for the surrender hammered out.[7] On July 16th, Micklegate bar was opened, and the Royalist garrison of the city marched out on the first leg of its journey towards Skipton Castle, Sir

130

Henry Slingsby with them. These were the men who had elected to go on fighting, although some of the garrison and its commanders chose this moment to lay down their arms and to make their peace with the Parliament. On the night of the 16th/17th the Royalists slept at Hessay, and continued their journey towards Knaresborough on the morning of the 17th, skirting the edge of the battlefield which must have looked much as it had done a month before, a flat waste overlooked by a ridge line under corn. Only now, of course, that ridge line was a trampled, brutalised mess of crushed crops and mud. This was the second direct result of Marston Moor, the surrender of York, made doubly symbolic by the fact that it was to save York from enemy occupation that Rupert had made his great march in May and June, which was to be brought to a splendid conclusion by the destruction of the Allied armies.

The north of England henceforth, more or less, was the domain of Scottish soldiers and Lord Fairfax's army. The army of the Eastern Association moved off after York fell, southwards. A handful of Royalist garrisons maintained a token presence. Scarborough under Cholmeley, Pontefract under Richard Lowther, Skipton under Sir John Mallory, Bolton Castle under John Scrope, and Helmsley Castle under Sir Jordan Crossland. One by one these were reduced, Skipton not for another 18 months, Pontefract and Scarborough not for a year. Sir Thomas Glemham, unable to hold York, took command in Carlisle and showed the Scottish army what he could do with a determined garrison. At Newcastle-upon-Tyne, however, in October, the Scottish siege army stormed and took the town amidst very heavy fighting, and North-umberland and Durham were lost to the King from then on.

The third result of Marston Moor was, therefore, the almost complete loss of northern England to the King. Yet this was by no means a foregone conclusion, for the Allied forces did not set about a systematic occupation of the whole area – logistics precluded this – and, in consequence, Newcastle's old cavalry on two separate occasions brought a good deal of anxiety and trouble to Lord Fairfax, with his headquarters in York. The loss of the north was potentially reversible, and had it been practicable for the King to attempt this reverse, the military consequences of Marston Moor could have been confined to Newcastle's departure and the temporary loss of York, even though Rupert chose on July 4th to abandon it all.

When Rupert marched away from York on July 4th Cholmeley

reckoned his total army at 4,000 men, whilst Slingsby said that he took with him as 'many of his footmen as he could force'. These cannot have been more than a few hundred. Watson gave Rupert's cavalry as 2,000 strong, Clarke as 3,000 but 'not any foote lefte'. With the accession of Clavering's men, who came to him somewhere between Thirsk and Richmond, the total force at the prince's disposal must have been in the region of 5,000, mostly horse. This army was rapidly fragmented, however. Goring and Clavering were detached to Carlisle, whilst Colonel Sir John Mayney, returning from his escort duties, was sent into Furness in Lancashire to recruit there. As the army moved on through Lancashire, Molyneux and Tyldesley were likewise sent off to try to bring up recruits. On July 6th, Rupert was joined at Richmond by the Marquess of Montrose,[8] who, after discussions the details of which have not been recorded, took Clavering's force away with him and, accompanied by Goring, made for Carlisle. Clavering died en route, but his regiment passed to the Durham catholic, John Forcer, who was henceforth to command it to effect. At Bolton Castle on the 7th, Henry Chaytor who had fought in the Royalist centre on Marston Moor was put with his men into the garrison to strengthen it, and his departure must have accounted for such infantry as Rupert had at his disposal, or a good part of them. The first actual confrontation between Royalist cavalry and some Scots after the battle occurred at Preston Underscarr in the North Riding, where Mayney, on his way to join Rupert, beat up some Scottish cavalry on or around July 6th.[9]

Retracing his steps through Lancashire with some hesitancy, Rupert made his painful progress back south. Reaching Preston on July 10th, he turned back north and established himself at Kirby Lonsdale from July 18th to July 20th. Precisely why he was hesitating is not clear: he might have expected word from Montrose in Carlisle, but it is more probable that he was awaiting the results from Sir John Mayney's attempt to recruit fresh forces in Furness. On the 17th or 18th of July, Mayney, venturing into this fairly solidly Royalist area of north Lancashire in the company of its leading local squire, Colonel Sir John Preston (who had fought on Marston Moor in the Northern Horse), found considerable Parliamentarian activity, and had to fight his way to Preston's home at Dalton. Although Mayney won the action,[10] it showed that nothing was going to be very straight-forward. Advised also of the surrender of York, Rupert now set his face solidly south. He was in

Liverpool on July 23rd, and in Chester on the 25th. Sir Thomas Fairfax, on July 30th, informed the Committee of Both Kingdoms in London that at this stage, Rupert had only 2,000 men with him,[11] and that the forces left behind in north Lancashire under Mayney, and at Carlisle under Montrose and Goring, were enough of a danger for a body of the Scottish army to be sent to deal with them. This was confirmed by the Earl of Manchester in another despatch. Parliament's commanders in Cheshire, however, stated that on August 1st Rupert had no fewer than 5,800 men at his immediate disposal,[12] whilst the Committee in London, sifting reports, wrote of 9,000 'very active and of great power'.[13] Rupert's presence could still, apparently, evoke either foreboding doom, despite Marston Moor, or draw forces to him when he needed them. So contradictory, however, are the Parliamentarian sources when dealing with the prince's strength, that it is impossible to be sure of their precise number or composition.

The Royalist forces which had marched out of York on July 16th began to break up on or around the 18th at Knaresborough. According to Sir Henry Slingsby, some elected to take the shortest way to join up with Rupert, while others chose to go with Sir Thomas Glemham towards Carlisle, like Slingsby himself. At Kirby Lonsdale on July 24th they met up with Sir Marmaduke Langdale who was also trying to recruit new forces in Westmorland and raise much needed money. Slingsby then parted from Glemham, and made his way with a few companions to Furness to join Mayney. In the month after Marston Moor Rupert's army was badly disorganised. He permitted it to be divided partly to satisfy Montrose and partly to beat the drum for recruits in the villages and towns of north-west England. Since this fragmentation began as early as July 6th it is hard to see that Rupert truly intended to make a second attempt to relieve York, although the Allies feared this and the garrison of York hoped for it. The abandonment of the north was an implicit acceptance that, with the departure of Newcastle and his commanders, the north was already lost. What is plain is that Rupert caused it to become so by dissipating his forces and showing, in the aftermath of a serious defeat, a considerable degree of hesitancy and doubt. York's surrender on July 16th was partially forced upon Glemham by conditions in the town and by the morale of the soldiers, but plenty of these were willing to go on fighting as is evident from their choice to march out and to seek employment elsewhere under the royal standard. There was still some resilience amongst the Royalists of the north, but Rupert made no attempt to capitalise upon it. If he is not to blame for the defeat on Marston Moor, he was surely guilty of the loss of the north.

Mayney's brigade took shape again in Furness, including in its strength what was left of the regiment of Colonel William Eure which had been badly damaged on Marston Moor,[14] now commanded by its major, Robert Busbridge.[15] What befell this brigade, crucial both to the later history of a part of the Royalist cavalry which escaped Marston Moor, and also to the view that the north was by no means completely lost, is recounted both by Slingsby himself and by Mayney's anonymous chronicler.[16] On July 24th, when Rupert was at Liverpool, Mayney had to fight again at Cartmell where he won a valuable victory. He took 'five waggon-loads of Arms from the said Enemy, with which he armed a Regiment of Foot which he raised there: in which service he was hurt and his horse shot dead under him'. These were the type of results that Rupert needed, but it seems that despite Mayney's success and recruitment drive, Rupert, although sent prisoners by Mayney with news of his actions, did not bother to order these fresh forces up to him. As far as Rupert was concerned, the fall of York had deprived all further activity in the north of any practical value. Mayney's isolation, and the use to which he ultimately turned it, robbed a remarkable achievement of any long-term significance. Sir John increased his assets by ransoming some of the Lancashire Parliamentarian gentry whom he had captured, and set about turning the Dalton area into a Royalist stronghold. He launched an attack on Walney Island, garrisoned by local Parliamentry levies who watched his activities without interfering. The projected assault failed and Mayney himself was again wounded, but the threat was sufficient, and Walney was abandoned by its garrison. Given a free hand Sir John used his soldiers to extract rents due to the King, and in this fashion raised in excess of £2,000, half of which he sent to Carlisle to be employed by Glemham, in paying the soldiers who were daily expecting to be besieged by the Scots.

These activities took up much of August, whilst the brigade was

134

offered 'open house' by Thomas Preston the squire of Holker, Slingsby noting

> a house free for all comers, & no grudging at any Cost, tho' we eat him up
> at his table; & ye Troopers in ye feild, stealing his sheepe, & not sparing
> his corn yt stood in ye feild; and here we took our pastime, & would go
> out to hunt and course ye dear. . . .

Yet there was a limit to such localised successes, and a danger in merely staying put. Mayney and his commanders debated how best to turn their strength to good account, and some – officers from Earnley's regiment at Marston Moor – wanted to make contact with Rupert. Being informed from Carlisle that Glemham could offer no forage or support for a cavalry force, Mayney decided to return to Yorkshire, and on September 10th the brigade, with Preston, made their way towards Skipton Castle. The decision to leave was probably partly inspired by events elsewhere in Lancashire.

Sir John Meldrum had been reinforced by contingents of the Lancashire forces which had done so badly at Marston Moor, and on August 10th began to move out from the town of Manchester to deal with those forces left behind in the county by Rupert.[17] That Meldrum should have received reinforcements was a reflection of the fear in York that something was afoot against the Allied dominance in Yorkshire. 'It is not improbable that such a design is on foot',[18] wrote Lord Fairfax from York on August 12th, and alluded to at least 3,000 cavalry reported to be in Cumberland under Langdale. It is a credit to Newcastle's old horse regiments that Lord Fairfax in the flush of victory should have betrayed such fear of them. Meldrum, whose orders were to disrupt Royalist recruitment in Lancashire, intended to force Molyneux, General Byron and Tyldesley from the Amounderness and Fylde areas. On August 15th and 16th the cavalry actions of Ribble Bridge and Walton Cop were fought. At Ribble Bridge a surprise confrontation led to a Royalist victory but reserves came to the aid of the Parliamentarians, and the situation was reversed on the 16th.[19] Four days later, at Ormskirk, Meldrum himself struck the bulk of the Marston Moor cavalry then in Lancashire. By this time, Tyldesley, Molyneux and Byron had been joined by George Goring and Langdale from Carlisle; their cavalry had been sent away by Glemham in advance of a siege; Meldrum, in reporting his victory, gave the Royalist strength at 2,500 cavalry and 200 foot. These were hopelessly scattered by

Meldrum's attack, a hundred were killed and a further 300 taken prisoners, while it was rumoured that Tyldesley himself had been killed.[20] Royalist sources imply that Langdale considered Byron's dispositions to have been at fault, and instrumental in allowing Meldrum so complete a rout as he achieved over forces strung out in column of march. The result of the action was that much Royalist recruitment had been squandered and Mayney, up in Furness, was now decidedly isolated.

Parliamentarian military operations in Yorkshire, the county to which Mayney's brigade began to return on September 10th, had, after Marston Moor been primarily concerned with the reduction of minor Royalist garrisons. On July 26th the first of these, Tickhill Castle, which preyed upon the trade of the Halifax area, fell to Eastern Association forces under Henry Ireton.[21] On the following day, the Earl of Manchester summoned the garrison of Sheffield to surrender,[22] a summons defied by the garrison commander, Thomas Beaumont of Whitley. Lawrence Crawford, the successful infantry commander from Marston Moor, appeared before Sheffield on August 4th and issued a sterner summons but Beaumont withdrew into the castle and gave up the town to the enemy, who promptly occupied it. The fighting here was not severe, although Royalist elements skirmished in the town,[23] and Beaumont surrendered on terms on August 11th. By August 22nd, Lord Fairfax was able to report from York that his forces were now besieging the castles of Knaresborough, Pontefract, Scarborough and Helmsley, but had to admit that he did not entertain any great hopes of immediate success.[24] At Pontefract the Royalist garrison resisted staunchly, launching cavalry raids from within the walls with startling effect.[25] Moreover, Pontefract was the objective of Mayney's brigade.

The Royalist horse, driving with them a thousand head of cattle, made first for Skipton where Mayney delivered part of the herd for the garrison. From there, apparently unobserved by any enemy patrols, he began a direct march for Pontefract which he reached on September 14th or 15th. Near Bradford, according to Slingsby,[26] they came upon 'a new rais'd Troop' which they dispersed, taking several prisoners. Apparently this encounter provided the besiegers of Pontefract with the first news which they had of Mayney's approach, and Slingsby believed that the tale grew in the telling, so that the Parliamentarian commander was under the impression that the brigade was 'ye prince's horse, & a

136

greater number y^n we were'. It may be considered a measure of the lack of confidence which the Yorkshire Parliamentary commanders felt, regardless of their victory on Marston Moor and their capture of York, that so soon as a Royalist force, however numerically small, made a firm offensive drive into their territory, there was panic. The Parliamentarian commander at Pontefract (Lambert, who had been there, does not appear to have been there when Mayney came into view) sent word to Lord Fairfax at York and begged for reinforcements. Fairfax, however, who in mid-August had been fretting about the possibility of Prince Rupert's return, was prepared to take no chances, and commanded the siege forces to withdraw. They reckoned, however, without Mayney's determination to force a battle. Although the brigade approached by way of Bradford and Castleford, and the Parliamentary forces were drawn up at Brotherton away to the north, Mayney moved too fast for them. 'He engaged, and fought them, and beat them, and had pursuit of them sixteen miles, and took and killed above five hundred of their men besides Officers, and took six of their Colours'.[27] Slingsby, who fought in the action, wrote:

> The enemy was drawn out on ye other side of ye bridge towards pomfret; Sr John sends a part to charge, & beats ym off their ground by ye help of ye foot soulgiers. They retreat beyond ye bridge, & would make good ye bridge; but Sr John's men animated seeing ym forsake their ground, comes wth more courage. The bridge had a Turnpike over ye middle of it, wch they had fasten'd. Our men allights from their horses, takes out of a Smith's shop a Hammer or such an Instrument, & breaks open ye Turnpike.

The sense of exhilaration on the part of the Royalists, scattering and decisively beating regiments which they had last encountered at Marston Moor, must have been considerable. Lord Fairfax, excusing the defeat which his men had sustained, informed the Committee of Both Kingdoms in London that Mayney's attack had been totally unexpected; and, at the same time, ordered troops away from other sieges to send them against Mayney.[28]

Mayney himself was seriously wounded in the fighting, and obliged to yield command of his brigade to Slingsby, Preston and Samuel Tuke,[29] who had fought on the Royalist right wing on Marston Moor. It was resolved that while Slingsby would remain behind with Mayney, Preston and Tuke would take the brigade on to Newark on Trent, the

137

major Royalist garrison in Nottinghamshire. After eight weeks, which time it took for Mayney to recover his health, he and Slingsby followed in the wake of the brigade.[30]

To claim that the Mayney raid was anything other than a minor achievement in the course of the civil war would be wrong. Yet it was significant in several respects. Mayney had, in Furness, showed that it was possible to recruit and to find funds with which to prosecute the war in the north. Faced by Rupert's abandonment of the northern counties he was able to drive a herd of cattle, with few more than a 1,000 cavalry, across the length of the West Riding of Yorkshire, supply Skipton with fresh meat 'on the hoof', secure tactical triumphs in the cloth towns heartland of Parliamentary recruiting, and then inflict a fairly devastating defeat upon a force of 2,000 to 3,000 Parliamentary troops at Pontefract. His raid increased Lord Fairfax's nervousness, and indicated what could be achieved even after so thorough a defeat as Marston Moor had been. In fact, all that the Royalist cavalry secured was a degree of recompense for their defeat on July 2nd, no small thing given the circumstances in which the raid was carried through. It would perhaps be piling on the irony to point out that at Pontefract on September 14th or 15th the Yorkshire Parliamentarian cavalry were put to flight by the same men who had put them to flight on July 2nd. It was probably a point which both sides more than appreciated.

When Mayney's brigade rode away southwards, there was thenceforth no Royalist field force of any description operative or potentially operative north of the River Trent. Cholmeley in Scarborough, Mallory in Skipton, might push raiding parties out and score minor victories, but between September and the following March of 1645, the north was the sole preserve of the Parliamentary and Scottish armies. The sieges dragged on. Sir Thomas Fairfax sustained a bullet wound at Helmsley that almost killed him. In siege warfare, given the failure of the Royalists to relieve their besieged comrades, time was always on the side of the besiegers.

The Royalist north was not lost to the King with Marston Moor and the fall of York, nor was it denied to him as minor garrisons fell towards the end of 1644. In March 1645 there was still opportunity, and would be for some months yet. As it was, Charles finally turned north when he was so weakened that he could not effectively influence events and the way which Mayney and others had shown was never properly followed or even understood. The Marquess of Newcastle's old cavalry, the Northern Horse, did return to their native counties, twice, in 1645, and faced again the Scottish and Parliamentarian cavalry which they had routed on Marston Moor. In their first encounter, in March, the Northern Horse rounded off a brilliant cavalry campaign with a second relief of Pontefract. Their second and last encounter came in October, after Naseby had depleted their numbers and undermined their morale and after the King had imposed upon them a courtier as their general. In October 1645 the Northern Horse went down at Sherburn in Elmet in Yorkshire and at Burgh-by-Sands in Cumberland. With their destruction, Newcastle's army was truly at an end.

After extricating his cavalry from the defeat at Ormskirk in August 1644, Sir Marmaduke Langdale, henceforth the commander-in-chief of the Northern Horse, built up their strength and morale. Fighting alongside the cavalry of the Oxford army, the Northern Horse, exciting both admiration and jealousy, nevertheless kept their eyes on events north of the Trent. Convinced of their own superiority, and drilled by Langdale, of whose martial qualities Slingsby was unstinting in his praise, by February 1645 these cavalry believed that they could win the north back to the King. If not mutinous, they were certainly restive, and with or without Langdale's knowledge, presented the King with a petition which, couched in submissive terms, would brook no argument:

> seeing our native counties as valuable and considerable, as we conceive, as any other parts of your Majesty's dominions, lieth enthralled under the pressures and insolencies of the enemy, and seeing the care and cure of those countries is no less your Majesty's work than the preservation of these, and in justice and charity, ought to be our endeavour before any other undertaking, and seeing that Pontefract and Carlyle . . . wherein are shut up most of the faithful and powerful gentry of those countries [are] straitly besieged if not distressed. . . . If we be wanting any longer to afford them that relief to which . . . we stand engaged, we shall render our case desperate by disenabling ourselves and party there from all such services.[31]

They therefore sought the King's 'consent, encouragement and assistance' to facilitate their 'march into the North, where we are constantly resolved to venture our dearest blood'. The narrowness of the Oxford Council of War's outlook certainly precluded any general movement north, as did the military situation in general early in 1645, but the petition was an attempt to widen the field of vision. That it was seriously

139

considered when it was so obviously critical of the King and of his advisors stresses the value of Langdale's cavalry. With his assistance a compromise was reached and the Northern Horse given leave to seek to relieve Pontefract but to go no further.

The great relief ride began somewhere near Oxford in mid-February. The northern cavalry rode so fast that they outstripped all news of their approach sent by one startled Parliamentarian commander to another along their route. As late as March 4th, three days after the relief was carried out, a correspondent in London wrote to tell Lord Fairfax at York that 'We hear of Sr M. Langdale's going northwards, with 2,000 horse, which I hope is no news to you.'[32] On February 28th, Sir Samuel Luke the vigilant governor of Newport Pagnell, wrote: 'I had word . . . this party of horse . . . are certainly to join with Prince Maurice, also, which to me seems a riddle because when they were at Chipping Norton [having arrived there from Salisbury] they were as near Shrewsbury as they were to Newark whither it [now] seems they are going.'[33] Luke, two days after Pontefract was relieved, was confused: 'which way they be rid is uncertain'.[34]

Leaving Banbury on February 23rd, the Northern Horse fought their first battle at Northampton, routing and killing some enemy horse.[35] On the 25th, they collided with a substantial Parliamentarian cavalry force at Melton Mowbray, the two sides of equal numbers, perhaps a little more than 2,000 on the enemy side.[36] Although the Royalists here lost Colonel Sir John Gerlington, former High Sheriff of Lancashire, they broke the Parliamentary force in the field and scattered it beyond immediate repair. On the 26th the brigade was four miles north of Newark, where they were reinforced by about 800 men from that garrison for the last leg of the journey. On March 1st, 1,500 Parliamentarian troops tried to block their path at Wentbridge near Pontefract, but fell back onto their main body which numbered, so the sources suggest, 2,500 foot and nearly 4,000 cavalry. On the afternoon of March 1st, the brigade came in view of this larger army, causing one of Langdale's commanders to write later, 'methought we viewed them with the fancy of that great Captaine when he first encountered Elephants'. the action proper began at about 6:00 in the evening, the Parliamentarian infantry opening fire from the shelter provided by a hedgerow, but hereupon the garrison of Pontefract sallied to support Langdale, and the Royalist charge was pressed home. Nathan Drake, diarist of the siege, and perhaps one of those who sallied forth, remembered:

> the horse charging with [our] foot four or five times, recovring the hedge from them, beat them quite away towards Ferry bridge, continually charging them all the way, there being left dead and wounded upon the ground about 160 men. And at Ferry bridge the Enemy played 3 times with one cannon, viz. 2 case shottes and 1 cannon bullit, killed there 4 of our men, but we bett them from their cannon, and tooke it. . . and followed them in chase betwixt Shearburne and Tadcaster, killd 140 of their men . . . in the chase, took 600 prisoners, commaunders and officers 57; doble barrells of powder 47, armes 1600, collores for horse and foot above 40; and many wounded men brought and many dead since.[37]

The Parliamentarians themselves testified to the complete rout of their forces under Lambert, a re-fighting of the encounter at Atterwith Lane eight months previously.[38] Pontefract was victualled, supplied with arms and captured powder, and for three or four days while the Pontefract garrrison roamed at will around the countryside, one local Parliamentarian officer confessed he 'scarce knew whither to turn'.

The relief of Pontefract was the last great exploit of the Northern Horse. Three months later, on Naseby field, they were routed by the cavalry of the New Model Army commanded by Oliver Cromwell, and the prestige attaching to their rapid ride of February and March was tarnished. In July, both Pontefract and Scarborough surrendered to the Parliament, after bitter siege warfare that saw the deaths, in Scarborough, of several veterans of Marston Moor. Nevertheless, Langdale had demonstrated the vulnerability of the north and the resolution of his cavalry on their home ground, and it was ironic that when, in August 1645, the King with an army of only 2,200 cavalry and 400 foot, turned north to recruit, it was far too late. The last Royalist garrisons in Yorkshire, Skipton and Bolton Castles and Sandal near Wakefield, the last of minor importance, were solidly invested now and the withdrawal of forces from the siege lines to deal with the King's northward march did not lead to any Royalist resurgence. On August 15th the King was at Staveley House in Derbyshire, where he was reinforced by approximately 2,000 horse and dragoons from Newark.[39] 'It is supposed they intend for Halifax and so northwards' a correspondent wrote to Lord Fairfax. On the 19th, the Royal army entered Doncaster, but on the 20th turned back into Nottinghamshire, went to Newark on the 21st, and so away south. It was an abortive manoeuvre of a beaten army. All the plans of the King and of his ebullient adviser George Digby to recruit a new army in the north came to nothing.[40] Faced by a concerted enemy movement, including 5,000 under David Leslie, the Royalists could not hold their ground.[41] 'So leaving many a poor Man that had shewn his willingness to the King's Service, to the Mercy of the Rebels' the army retreated.

On September 24th, this army came to grief at Rowton Heath near Chester where the Northern Horse, now divided into two brigades under Langdale and another Marston Moor veteran, Sir William Blakiston, performed well but were unable to overcome considerable tactical disadvantages. In October, the King apparently resolved to push through to the north and effect a junction with the Marquess of Montrose in Scotland, where he was performing prodigiously. On October 13th however, while at Welbeck, the Nottinghamshire home of the Marquess of Newcastle, word was brought to the King of setbacks suffered by Montrose. Hesitant, the Royalist Council of War was nevertheless strongly urged by Langdale[42] that the northward march was not without value still. The King, reluctant to pursue the original idea, but in want of a better, consented to a plan that the Northern Horse – perhaps 600 or 700 of them – with some additional cavalry, should continue the march and assist in imposing the authority of the new Lieutenant General of the northern counties, George Digby. Digby's career as an advisor to the King had been remarkable chiefly for the poor quality of his advice. As a military commander, he was far the inferior of Langdale and of Blakiston, and probably no better than many of the Northern Horse commanders. Nevertheless, it was under Digby's aegis that the survivors of Marston Moor met their fate.

There was initially something of the atmosphere of the Pontefract feat, although this time the cavalry were tired and burdened with numerous defeats and failures. Setting off on October 14th, they put to the sword a Parliamentarian force at Cusworth, and early on the 15th, riding by way of Ferrybridge, attacked 800 enemy cavalry at Sherburn in Elmet, scattering them and taking numerous prisoners.[43] At this point, carried away with success, Digby paused, and gave opportunity for the cautious Colonel Copley, following in their rear, to catch up with the Royalists and to force them to battle on ground advantageous to the Parliament's cavalry. In his account of the battle, Copley put into the mouth of Langdale a speech delivered before action was joined that, if not accurate in detail, must have borne some relation to an attempt by the commander of the Northern Horse to spur his men on.

> Gentlemen, you are all gallant men, and have done bravely, but there are some that seeke to scandalize your gallantry for the losse of Naseby Field, but I hope you will redeem your reputation, and still maintain that gallant report which you ever had. I am sure you have done such businesses, as never have been done in any war with such a number. . . . I hope you are Gentlemen and that you will still maintain it, and redeem that which you have lost, For mine owne parte, I will not have you upon any designe, but where I will lead you myselfe. . . .

This speech signals an inevitable development within warfare. The Northern Horse were not about to fight for Digby or with Digby, or, indeed, in the context of any general Royalist strategy. They were the Northern Horse, they were Langdale's. That was what they now fought as and for: survival.

The 'raging enemy', as a Parliamentarian commander described them, were defeated. Langdale's men cleared one of Copley's wings from the field, but reserves brought up gave Copley the numerical superiority he needed and turned possible rout into victory. The gentlemen and officers of the Northern Horse fought with courage, as Copley himself admitted, but they were simply overwhelmed. It was at Sherburn in Elmet that Colonel Francis Carnaby, who had returned from temporary exile with the Marquess of Newcastle, and who had held a command on the Royalist left wing on Marston Moor, was killed. Several other veterans of that battle were also casualties of this encounter, and only 300 cavalry, as the enemy reckoned, escaped. On the field the victorious Parliamentarians picked up the discarded colours of the regiments of Clavering and Carnaby.

The fugitives reached Skipton Castle, where Mallory offered them reinforcements and shelter.[44] From there, they pushed on into Lancashire by way of Kirby Lonsdale, and with the assistance of a local Royalist guide, evaded parties of Scottish and Parliamentary horse seeking them. So efficient was this guide that the Scots following lost all contact with the 'nimble brigade' when they turned north into Westmorland and so on towards the border at Carlisle. Colonel Sir John Brown, however, stumbled upon the Royalists at Burgh-by-Sands and, outnumbering them by two to one, charged them at once. The 'battle' was the merest formality. The Northern Horse were broken in spirit and in numbers, and they broke at Brown's first onslaught.[45] Langdale and

Digby escaped, and found refuge in the Isle of Man where the Earl of Derby doggedly refused to hand them over to the authorities. This was the end of Newcastle's army.

CONCLUSION

Few battles have any all-embracing consequences. Marston Moor wrecked the northern infantry, but the Northern Horse survived, though badly depleted thanks to Cromwell's manoeuvre, and demonstrated for almost a year afterwards that they were not to be discounted. The relief of Pontefract in September 1644 and in March 1645 demonstrated the capacity of the Royalists to exploit Parliamentarian uncertainty in the north, but these were all empty gestures in the context of such overall strategy as the King and Prince Rupert subscribed to. The north was thrown away because of Marston Moor and the fall of York, it was not won outright by the Allied armies. At Sherburn in Elmet and at Burgh-by-Sands, the uncompleted work of Marston Moor was brought to completion. Yet the overwhelming impression of the 15 months after Marston Moor, insofar as the north was concerned, is one of neglected opportunities. The psychological impact of that defeat on July 2nd 1644 on the Royalist party in general was as deep as that of Rupert's relief march in May and June had been upon the enemy in his line of march. Meldrum in June had insisted Rupert could be stopped with a little determination. Mesmerised, his superiors did not listen. Langdale had insisted the north was recoverable. No one really listened to him. It was a long way and a long ride from Marston Moor to Bugh-by-Sands, a long time of hope and frustration. Had it not been Burgh-by-Sands some other place would have come to symbolise the last military consequence of Marston Moor.

NOTES

1. *Calendar of State Papers*, Domestic Series, 1660/1, p. 205.
2. Clay, J. W., ed; *William Dugdale's Visitation of Yorkshire with Additions*, Exeter 1894–1917, Vols. III, p. 199; IV, p. 361.
3. Day, W. A., ed: *The Pythouse Papers*, 1879, pp. 22/3.
4. Schofield, B., ed: *The Knyvett Letters 1620–1644*, Norfolk Record Society, Vol. XX, 1949, p. 165.

5. HMC 9th Report 1883, Pt. II, Morrison Mss., p. 436.
6. Warburton, *Memoirs of Prince Rupert*, II, p. 433. The bulk of Rupert's army marched off during the 3rd, Rupert himself following it seems, early on the 4th.
7. British Library Thomason Tract, T.T. E 4 (6) 'A Continuation of True Intelligence'. Wenham, *Siege of York*, pp. 93/5.
8. Buchan, J., *Montrose*, 1928, p. 146.
9. Mayney Services, op. cit., Alnwick Castle Archives, f. 181.
10. *Ibid.*
11. *Calendar of State Papers, Domestic Series* 1644, p. 385.
12. *Ibid.*, p. 392.
13. *Ibid.*, p. 375.
14. Parsons, *Slingsby Diary*, pp. 122/4.
15. Robert Busbridge came, interestingly, from Harmer in Sussex, and had clearly joined the regiment when it served with the Oxford army in 1643.
16. *Slingsby Diary*, pp. 124/31. Mayney Services, f. 181.
17. Beamont, W.,ed: *A Discourse of the Warr in Lancashire*, Chetham Society, Old Series, Vol. LXII, 1864, p. 59.
18. *Calendar of State Papers, Domestic Series* 1644, p. 422.
19. Rushworth, J., *Historical Collections . . . 1618–1649*, 1659–1701, Vol. III, II, p. 745. Ormerod, G., ed: *Tracts Relating to Military Proceedings in Lancashire During the Great Civil War*, Chetham Society Old Series, Vol. II, 1844, pp. 204/5. Beamont, *Discourse of the Warr*, p. 59.
20. Ormerod, *Tracts*, p. 76. Beamont, *Discourse of the Warr*, pp. 55/9. Vicars, *Parliamentary Chronicles*, III, p. 12. British Library T.T. E 7 (25) 'A True Relation of two great Victories'. Warburton, *Memoirs of Prince Rupert*, III, pp. 21/2.
21. Vicars, *Parliamentary Chronicles*, II, pp. 293/4. *Calendar of State Papers, Domestic Series* 1644, p. 380.
22. Gatty, A., ed: *Joseph Hunter's Hallamshire*, 1869, p. 141. Vicars, *Parliamentary Chronicles*, III, pp. 7/8.
23. British Library T.T. E 8 (4) 'Journal of the Earl of Manchester's Army'.
24. *Calendar of State Papers, Domestic Series* 1644, p. 447.
25. British Library T.T. E 8 (22) 'A Copy of a Letter from the Lord General'.
26. *Slingsby Diary*, pp. 130/4.
27. Mayney Services, f. 181.
28. *Calendar of State Papers, Domestic Series* 1644, p. 520.
29. Tibbutt, H. G., ed: *The Letter Books 1644–45 of Sir Samuel Luke*, 1963, p. 339.
30. Warburton, *Memoirs of Prince Rupert*, I, p. 522. Mayney was still in Pontefract on October 12th on which day he wrote to Rupert.
31. *Ibid.*, III. pp. 70/1.
32. Bell, R., ed: *Memorials of the Civil War. Fairfax Correspondence*, 1849, Vol. I, pp. 166/7, 182/3. Bell's work is extremely valuable as a source, but a prime example of 19th century Whig interpretation.
33. Tibbutt, *Luke Letter Books*, p. 169.
34. *Ibid.*, p. 175.
35. Whitelock, Bulstrode, *Memorials of the English Affairs*, 1682, p. 129.
36. *Ibid.*, p. 130. Tibbutt, *Luke Letter Books*, p. 217. Warburton, *Memoirs of Prince Rupert*, III, pp. 67/8.
37. Longstaffe, W. H. D., ed: Nathan Drake's Journal of the First and Second Sieges of Pontefract Castle 1644–5, *Surtees Society*, Vol. XXXVII, Pt. 1, Miscellanea, 1861, p. 14.
38. Hodgson, Captain John, *Memoirs*, Bradford Antiquary, New Series, Pt. XII, 1908, pp. 144/5. Bell, *Fairfax Correspondence*, I, pp. 177/8.
39. HMC 13th Report, Appendix Pt. 1, Portland Mss., 1891, pp. 253/4.
40. *Calendar of State Papers, Domestic Series* 1645/7, pp. 70/1.
41. Vicars, *Parliamentary Chronicles*, III, pp. 258/9.

42. Walker, Sir Edward, *Historical Discourses upon Several Occasions*, 1705, pp. 135, 144.
43. Whitelock, *Memoirs*, p. 162. Vicars, *Parliamentary Chronicles*, III, pp. 297/9.
44. Leeds City Library Archives, Vyner Manuscripts, 5815 T/32/42.
45. Vicars, *Parliamentary Chronicles*, III, pp. 306/309. British Library T.T. E 308 (7) The Routing of the Lord Digby; and T.T. E 308 (8) A True Relation of the Totall Routing of the Lord George Digby.

BIBLIOGRAPHY

Battle Sources

This bibliography is arranged alphabetically first citing the abbreviated form by which the source is alluded to in the text. Other contemporary sources not so alluded to because they offer nothing of moment and are either pure propaganda or obvious compilations, are indicated by an asterisk. The abbreviation T.T. means that the source cited is in the British Library, Thomason Tract collection.

* *A Dog's Elegy*, T.T. E 3 (17)
* *A Particular List of the Officers taken prisoners at Marston Moor*, T.T. E 54 (8)
* *A True Relation of the late fight*, T.T. E 54 (7)
ASHE Simeon: *A Continuation of True Intelligence*, T.T. E 2 (1), July 10.
BOWLES, Edward: *Manifest Truths*, 1646, T.T. E 343 (1)
CHOLMELEY, Sir Hugh: 'Memorials touching the battle of York', *English Historical Review*, V, 1890, pp. 347/352.
CLARKE, Robert: to Captain Bartlett, letter of July 14, Carte Mss. xi 444, printed in C. H. Firth, 'Marston Moor', *Transactions of the Royal Historical Society*, New Series, Vol. XII, 1898, pp. 76/9.
DE GOMME, Sir Bernard: 'Order of His Majties Armee', British Library Additional Ms. 16370, f. 64. Printed by Firth in his 'Marston Moor' *op. cit.*, and by Peter Young, *Marston Moor*, 1970, plate 22.
DESPATCH: Allied Generals' Despatch of July 5th, *Calendar of State Papers, Domestic Series* 1644, p. 311.
DIARY: 'The Rupert Diary', Wiltshire County Record Office, printed by Young, *op. cit.*, pp. 212/3.
DOUGLAS, Robert: 'Diary', in *Historical Fragments, relative to Scottish Affairs from 1635 to 1664*, Edinburgh 1833. Also given in C. S. Terry, *Life and Campaigns of Alexander Leslie*, 1899, pp. 280/3.
FAIRFAX, Sir Thomas: 'A Short Memorial of the Northern Actions', *Yorkshire Archaeological Journal*, Vol. VIII, 1884, pp. 220/222. Also printed in Firth, C. H., ed: *Stuart Tracts 1603–93*, 1903; J. Horsfall Turner, *The Old History of Bradford*, Idel, 1894. An early edition is B. Fairfax, ed: *A Short Memoriall of the Northern Actions*, 1699.
GRIFEN, Robert: letter of July 3, in T.T. E 2 (14) – see WATSON.
LILLY/CAMBY: William Lilly, *History of his Life and Times*, 1826 edn., pp. 77/8, but all editions contain this account.
LUDLOW, Edmund: C. H. Firth, ed: *The Memoirs of Edmund Ludlow*, Oxford 1894, pp. 98/100. The original edition is Vivay, Switzerland, 1698, Vol. I, pp. 123/5.
LUMSDEN, Sir James: Letter to Lord Loudon and Allied Battle Plan, York Minister Library, July 5th. Printed in Young, *op. cit.*, plate 21.
MONCKTON, Sir Philip: 'Memoir', printed in Firth, op. cit., pp. 52/3. Also in *Annual Register*, 1805, p. 883; Young, *op. cit.*, pp. 222/3.
NEWCASTLE MEMOIR: C. H. Firth, ed: *The Life of William Cavendish Duke of Newcastle*, n.d., pp. 37/41.
OGDEN: Mr. Ogden's letter to Sir Walter Wrottesley, July 5th, printed in Firth, op. cit., pp. 71/2.

SAVAGE: ? Savage's letter to Sir Philip Musgrave, Cumbria County Record Office, Carlisle, Musgrave Mss.

SAYE: Lord Saye & Sele, *Vindiciae Veritatis*, 1654, T.T. E 811 (2)

SHELLEY, Henry: letter to Sir Thomas Pelham. July 9, British Library Additional Ms. 33084, f. 67. Printed in Young, *op. cit.*, pp. 255/7.

SLINGSBY, Sir Henry: Parsons, D., ed: *Diary of Sir Henry Slingsby*, 1836.

SOMERVILLE, Lt. Colonel James: in James Lord Somerville's *Memorie of the Somervilles*, Edinburgh 1815, Vol. II, pp. 343/52. Also printed in Young, *op. cit.*, pp. 258/263.

STEWART, Captain William: *A Full Relation of the Victory Obtained*, T.T. E 54 (19), July 6. Printed in C.S. Terry, *Life of Leslie*, op. cit., pp. 274/80.

STOCKDALE, Thomas: letter to John Rushworth, July 5, British Library Harleian Ms. 166, f. 87. Printed in Firth, *op. cit.*, pp. 73/6; and in Young, *op. cit.*, pp. 234/8.

THORNTON, Mrs. Jackson, C.: ed: *The Autobiography of Mrs. Alice Thornton of East Newton, Co. York*, Surtees Society, Vol. LXIII, 1873, p. 44.

TREVOR, Arthur: letter to the Marquess of Ormond, July 10th, in Carte, T., ed: *A Collection of Original Letters and Papers*, 1739, Vol. I, pp. 55/8. Printed in Young, *op. cit.*, pp. 223/5.

*VICARS, John: *Parliamentary Chronicles*, 1646, Vol. II, p. 268 (based almost entirely upon Ashe, *q.v.*, *supra*.)

W. H.: *A Relation of the good successe*, c. July 3/4, T.T. E 54 (11). Printed in Young, *op. cit.*, pp. 246/9.

WATSON, Lionel: *A more exact Relation of the late Battell Neer York*, c. July 3, T.T. E 2 (14), published with GRIFEN (*q.v.*, *supra*). Printed in Young, *op. cit.*, pp. 227/32 and given there as T.T. E 100 (12).

WILLIAM FAIRFAX: in Markham, C., *Life of Robert Fairfax of Steeton*, 1885, pp. 19/20, letter of July 3.

See also Payne Fisher's poem *Marston Moor*, T.T. E 535.

SECONDARY ACCOUNTS

As will have been gathered, this present study of the battle disputes major points with all others previously written. Studies of the battle have been numerous, but few of any merit, the subject too often being merely the repetition of old ideas and interpretations. The following, mostly cited in the text, have certain peculiar merits as indicated.

BARRETT, C. R. B.: *Battles and Battlefields in England*, 1896, pp. 320/51. Barrett treated of 34 battles in this book, and thus the overall impression is one of thinness. However, he certainly visited the battlefield, and his text is embellished with pen and ink sketches of 'views', interesting but indicative to his approach. Nonetheless, he was sceptical about the tradition attaching to White Syke Close.

BURNE, A. H.: *The Battlefields of England*, 1950, pp. 221/30. Burne was a thoughtful researcher and his study of the battle's sources is good on the whole. He thought Barrett's work 'thoughtful', and himself entertained doubts concerning traditional ideas, but did not feel sure enough to pursue them.

FIRTH, C. H.: 'Marston Moor', *Transactions of the Royal Historical Society*, New Series, Vol. XII, 1898, pp. 17/79. Firth was a scholar of distinction, and although he apparently did not visit the battlefield, he treated the sources with clinical exactness. Dismissive of Stewart and too enamoured of de Gomme.

LEADMAN, A. D. H.: *Battles Fought in Yorkshire*, 1891, pp. 117/76. This work was composed from papers originally printed in the *Yorkshire Archaeological Journal*, without amendment or revision. Failure to even consider the implications of terrain is most evident, but there is a mass of detail, factual and mythological, interwoven with a patchy narrative of events. Leadman dismissed de Gomme but for the wrong reasons.

ROGERS, H. C. B.: *Battles and Generals of the Civil Wars*, 1968, pp. 136/51. Chiefly remarkable for the sustained dismissal of Cromwell as having any hand in the victory, an approach maintained throughout the book wherever Cromwell fought. Rogers' idea that Sir Thomas Fairfax won the battle is fallacious. One or two minor errors of fact.

TERRY, C. S.: *Life and Campaigns of Alexander Leslie*, 1899, pp. 219/83. Terry was an untiring pursuer of accuracy, and all of his work may still be studied with benefit by the student of the civil war, so that his neglect is unjustifiable. Professor Woolrych reckoned Terry's study of the battle invaluable, and within limitations, it may be considered to have been the best brief study until Burne.

WOOLRYCH, A. H.: *Battles of the English Civil War*, 1961, pp. 63/80. A concise enunciation of the traditional interpretation of events, but placed in the wider context of the war as a whole, an approach rarely adopted by others and extremely valuable regardless of the treatment of the actual battle. The best study since Burne.

YOUNG, P.: *Marston Moor*, 1970. The first monograph which the battle has merited, but description of the actual battle limited to pp. 107/42 out of virtually 300 pages all told. The book is crammed with valuable data concerning the rival armies, although that for the Marquess of Newcastle's army must be treated with extreme caution. A serious attempt to give the battle the treatment it rightly merits.

INDEX

151

Lifeguard, Prince Rupert's, 44, 72, 109, 113
Lilly, William, 5, 118, 120
Lincolnshire, 14, 20
Lindsay, John Lord, 108, 111, 113, 116, 117, 121
Linton, Kent, 6
Liverpool, Lancashire, 29, 133, 134
Livingstone, Alexander, 107
London, 7, 14, 24, 36, 54, 127, 133, 137, 140
Long Marston, Yorkshire, 7, 48, 49, 50, 51, 53, 54, 55, 56, 57, 91, 97, 101, 121, 125
Loudon, earl of, 108, 116
Loughborough, Henry Hastings, Lord, 24
Lowther, Richard, 131
Lucas, Sir Charles, 17, 18, 21, 22, 28, 36, 44, 91, 93, 98, 99, 103, 111, 115, 116, 117, 122, 124, 126
Lucas, Gervase, 23
Ludlow, Edmund, 5, 71, 100
Lumsden, Sir James, 5, 51, 55, 56, 62, 66, 89, 92, 95, 107, 108, 112, 113, 114, 116, 117
Luke, Sir Samuel, 140

Mackworth, Sir Francis, 20, 37, 42, 129
Maitland, see Lauderdale
Mallory, Sir John, 131, 138, 143
Malpas, Battle of, 126
Malton, Yorkshire, 21
Manchester, Lancashire, 28, 36, 135
Manchester, Edward Montague, earl of, 1, 2, 27, 35, 46, 51, 52, 56, 57, 61, 85, 97, 101, 107, 108, 111, 112, 113, 114, 122, 124, 126, 133, 136
Mansfield, Charles Cavendish, Viscount, 126
Marston Moor, topography of, 1, 2, 3, 43, 46f, 58, 61, 63, 92
Maurice, Prince, 140
Mayney, Sir John, 6, 19, 38, 44, 91, 109, 129, 130, 132, 133, 134, 136, 137, 138
Meldrum, Sir John, 24, 28, 29, 35, 36, 37, 38, 39, 135, 136, 144
Melton Mowbray, Leicestershire, 140
Metham, Sir Thomas, 44, 115, 124
Micklegate Bar, York, 38, 42, 49, 50, 65, 130
Middleton, Sir George, 22
Millward, John, 29, 109
Molyneux, Caryll, 79
Molyneux, Richard, Viscount, 58, 70, 78,

79, 80, 81, 82, 86, 87, 93, 98, 113, 127, 132, 135
Monckton, Sir Philip, 5, 66, 98, 102, 103, 121, 122, 128
Montrose, James Graham, Marquess of, 26, 27, 66, 132, 133, 142
Moor Lane, Marston Moor, see Sandy Lane
Moor Monckton, Yorkshire, 25, 125
Morpeth, Northumberland, 15, 26, 27
Musgrave, Sir Philip, 105, 121

Napier, Thomas, 70, 71, 72, 74, 75, 77, 79, 87, 89, 109, 111, 112
Naseby, Battle of, 126, 139, 141, 143
New Model Army, The, 2, 141
Newark on Trent, 16, 21, 23, 24, 137, 140, 141
Newcastle, Duchess of, 38, 39, 41, 60, 61, 64, 80, 118f, 120
Newcastle, William Cavendish, Marquess of, 6, 14f, 25f, 36, 38, 39, 40f, 58, 59, 60, 64, 65, 80, 81, 101, 104, 105, 113, 115, 116, 118, 119, 120, 122, 124, 126, 129, 130, 131, 133, 135, 139, 142, 143, 144
Newcastle, Marquess of, Army of, 15f, 36, 37, 38, 43, 101
Newcastle Memoirs, 5
Newcastle upon Tyne, City of, 14, 15, 17, 26, 27, 131
Newport Pagnell, Bedfordshire, 140
Nidd, River, 50
Northern Horse, The, 25, 27, 28, 29, 36, 42, 44, 91, 102, 103, 129, 130, 132, 135, 139f
Northumberland, 13, 14, 15, 17, 18, 20, 131
Nottinghamshire, 14, 23, 25, 138, 141, 142

Ogden, Mr., 5, 7, 64, 99, 113, 124, 128
Ormskirk, Battle of, 126, 135, 139
Otley, Yorkshire, 30
Ouse, River, 23, 30, 36, 42, 49, 56
Oxford Army, The, Royalist, 14, 20, 36, 139
Oxford, City of, 15, 18, 40, 140

Parliament, The, 13, 14
Parliament, The Army of the, 20, 22, 23, 24, 132, 137
Pelham, Sir Thomas, 7

154

Pennines, 20
Pickering, Yorkshire, 22
Piercebridge, Co. Durham, 118
Pontefract, Yorkshire, 25, 131, 136, 137, 138, 139, 140, 141, 142, 144
Poppleton, Yorkshire, 49, 124
Porter, George, 23, 24, 124
Preston, Sir John, 132, 135, 137
Preston, Thomas, 135
Preston, Lancashire, 132
Preston Underscarr, Yorkshire, 132

Quarrendon Hill, Co. Durham, 19

Rae, James, 108, 111
Ribble Bridge, Battle of, 135
Richmond, Yorkshire, 132
Rigby, Alexander, 28
Rogers, H. C. B., 2
Rowton Heath, Battle of, 142
Royalist Army, The, on Marston Moor, 34, 41, 42, 44, 46, 51, 56, 57, 58, 59, 62, 63, 64, 91, 92, 102, 103, 105, 108, 124
Rufforth, Yorkshire, 125
Rupert Diary, The, 5
Rupert, Prince, 1, 6, 13, 15, 19, 21, 23, 25f, 34, 36f, 54f, 58f, 64f, 70f, 78, 80, 83, 100, 102, 103, 108, 109, 111, 113, 115, 121, 124, 127f, 137, 138, 144
Rupert, Prince, Army of, 25, 27, 28, 29, 30, 34, 36, 42, 49, 55, 58, 70, 71, 132, 133, 135

Salisbury, Wiltshire, 140
Salvin, Francis, 101
Sandal Castle, Yorkshire, 141
Sandy Lane, Marston Moor, 50, 52, 58, 114, 121, 125
Savage, ?William, 5
Saville, Sir William, 20, 21
Saye and Sele, Lord, 5, 79, 85, 86
Scarborough, Yorkshire, 6, 7, 22, 25, 130, 131, 136, 138, 141
Scottish Army, 1 13f, 24, 27, 35, 56, 58, 71, 89, 96, 107, 132, 133, 138
Scrope, John, 131
Selby, Battle of, 1, 19, 23, 24, 25, 28, 37, 128
Selby, Yorkshire, 56
Sheffield, Yorkshire, 136
Shelley, Henry, 5, 7, 125, 127

Sherburn in Elmet, Battle of, 139,141f
Shrewsbury, Shropshire, 140
Skipton Castle, Yorkshire, 25, 30, 130, 131, 135, 136, 138, 141, 143
Slingsby, Sir Charles, 16, 126
Slingsby, Sir Henry, 5, 25, 38, 45, 52, 58, 59, 60, 63, 78, 98, 101, 117, 128, 130, 131, 132, 133, 134, 135, 136, 137, 138, 139
Somerville, James, 4, 5, 66, 86, 102, 119, 120, 128
South Cave, Yorkshire, 63
Staffordshire, 80
Stamford Bridge, Yorkshire, 21
Staveley, Derbyshire, 141
Stewart, William, 5, 6, 51f, 54, 56, 58, 71, 72, 92, 95, 96, 107, 112, 114, 117, 127
Stockdale, Thomas, 5, 34, 37, 57, 62, 63, 78, 96, 99, 114, 125, 127
Stockport, Cheshire, 28
Sunderland, Co. Durham, 17, 18, 27
Sweden, 78

Tadcaster, Yorkshire, 30, 56, 57, 60, 141
Tees, River, 19, 118
Tempest, Sir Richard, 109, 119, 127
Terry, C. S., 6
Thirsk, Yorkshire, 132
Thomlinson, John, 126
Thornhill, Yorkshire, 20
Thornton, Mrs. Alice, 5, 63, 120
Thwaites, Family of, 50
Tickhill Castle, Yorkshire, 136
Tillier, Henry, 109, 111, 114, 117, 121, 122, 124
Tockwith, Yorkshire, 48, 50, 51, 53, 54, 55, 97, 125
Topham, Henry, 101
Trained Bands, The, 15
Trent, River, 16, 138, 139
Trevor, Arthur, 5, 74, 95, 109, 124
Trevor, Marcus, 70, 79, 86, 109
Tuke, Samuel, 70, 75, 78, 79, 91, 137
Turner, Sir James, 16, 35
Tyldesley, Sir Thomas, 28, 70, 79, 109, 111, 127, 132, 135, 136
Tyne, River, 16, 17, 27
Tynemouth, Northumberland, 26

Urry, Sir John, see Hurry, Sir John

Vaughan, Sir William, 70, 79

155

156